Gloria D. Miklowitz

The War Between the Classes

Text and Study Aids
Edited and annotated
by Rudolph F. Rau

Ernst Klett Sprachen
Stuttgart

A Note on the Text

This edition of *The War Between the Classes* contains the complete and unabridged text of the original. American spelling conventions have been preserved and are also used in the annotations.

Annotations by Rudolph Franklin Rau, Weinstadt

1. Auflage 1 25 24 23 | 2014 13 12

Alle Drucke dieser Auflage sind unverändert und können im Unterricht nebeneinander benutzt werden. Die letzten Zahlen bezeichnen jeweils die Auflage und das Jahr des Druckes.

Internetadresse: www.klett.de / www.lektueren.com

Redaktion: Dr. Hartmut K. Selke
Umschlagfoto: shutterstock © John Bailey
Foto Umschlaginnenseite: © Arthur Montes de Oca 1988. All rights reserved.
Druck: CPI books GmbH, Leck
Printed in Germany.

ISBN 978-3-12-578110-8

9 783125 781108

Contents

How to Read an English Book Without a Dictionary

As a student of English you will already have discovered that reading an English book is not always an easy affair. Looking up words in a dictionary can be time-consuming and demotivating. However, you can overcome these obstacles if you use certain techniques which help you to guess the meaning of unknown words. Reading English can be an enjoyable rather than frustrating experience if you bear in mind the techniques described below.

1. Word Family
The meaning of unknown words can often be determined by identifying the *root word* and then finding out how the prefix or suffix changes its use or meaning. In the example "in disbelief" (**17** 8) the prefix "dis-" indicates that the opposite of "belief" is meant. This knowledge and the context in which "in disbelief" is used make the meaning quite clear. Or take "nursed" (**21** 17). You are familiar with the noun "a nurse". Here the word is obviously used as a verb and its meaning is easy to guess.

2. Similar German, French or Latin Words (Cognates)
Your own language or words you have learned in French or Latin can help you to discover the meaning of unknown English words. Take "privileges" (**34** 3) as an example. The German and Latin words are almost identical. Or take "in parting" (**10** 30), which may remind you of the French word "partir" in the sense of "to leave". The similarity of "swarming" (**8** 9) to the German "schwärmen" is self-evident.

3. Context
By looking carefully at the words or sentences before and after an unknown word or expression you can often discover its meaning. Examining the *context* in which a word appears is probably the best way of finding out the meaning of difficult words. Take the word "turmoil" (**7** 6) on the first page of the novel. The immediate context ("inner") shows us that this "turmoil" is going on inside the person who is telling the story. In the first paragraph she describes what is going on inside her: thousands of butterflies are "leaping and fluttering inside" her chest. "Turmoil," we may therefore conclude, must be a state of confusion, nervousness, and agitation. Or look at the word "handsome" (**12** 13). The context tells us that it must mean the exact opposite of "ugly" in the same line.

However, finding the meaning of a word is not always as simple as that, and sometimes you need the courage to make an *intelligent guess* after examining the larger context. Visualizing a whole scene can also help you to understand the meaning of unfamiliar words.

4. Sound (onomatopoeia)
Sometimes saying a word out loud will suggest its meaning. Refer to the word "mumble" in "the *mumble* of voices downstairs" (**7** 29). The word "mumble" when spoken out loud does sound like a lot of indistinct voices talking at the same time. Of course, the meaning of the word is also obvious from its context. As in this case, the four categories often overlap, and context is the most important among them.

Finally it is important to accept the fact that you will not understand every word when reading in a foreign language, or even in your own language. Don't let that frustrate you. You need not know every word to comprehend the general sense of a sentence or paragraph. Take the following sentence: "A pleasant block of *neatly* kept lawns ..." (**9** 1). You don't need to know what the adverb "neatly" means to understand the whole sentence (but you might be able to guess its meaning from the context).

It is a great achievement to read something in a foreign language on your own, without constantly having to refer to a dictionary. The words you know plus those explained at the bottom of each page will help you to understand most of this enjoyable novel. To give you an easy start, the words whose meanings can be discovered by using the techniques described above have been marked with a number in the first four chapters.

To summarize:
1 – words guessed from the word family (e.g. in disbelief[1])
2 – words guessed from similiar German, French or Latin words (e.g. in parting[2])
3 – words guessed from the context (e.g. turmoil[3])
4 – words guessed from the sound (e.g. mumble[4])

Biographical Note

Gloria D. Miklowitz has specialized in writing young adult novels that focus on important social issues such as AIDS, racial prejudice, and child abuse. Born in New York City in 1927, Gloria Miklowitz grew up in Brooklyn. After earning her M.A. in English at the University of Michigan in 1948, she married a college professor. For a time they lived in New Mexico and then finally settled in California. Now a widow, she resides in La Canada, California, has two sons, both college professors, and two granddaughters.

About her own motives for writing novels for young people:

I never thought, when I graduated from college, that I would write books, teach writing, speak at schools and conventions. It seems a miracle, but miracles are often self-made, I think. While some small talent is needed, it's only a small part of the recipe. A writer must also have curiosity, "sticking" power for the times when rejection comes, or when the story stalls, a fondness for words, and above all – when writing for children – a genuine love for and non-judgmental attitude towards the reader.

With regard to *The War Between the Classes* she has written:

I wrote The War Between the Classes *after reading about Prof. Otero's college class and contacting him for permission to sit in on the class , interview students and examine his workbooks. I knew instantly that his "game" was important in teaching tolerance for others and wanted to have teenagers examine their attitudes.*

Chapter 1

Butterflies. That's how I felt inside, like there were thousands of butterflies leaping and fluttering[2] inside my chest. Tonight was the dance, the luau, and I was going with Adam! He always says I seem so at peace with myself; if he only knew!

I pinned a red hibiscus[2] behind one ear and feathered[1] my long, straight hair out over my shoulders. No sign of the inner turmoil[3] in the mirror. All I saw was a slight flush on my cheeks and an extra brightness in my almond-shaped eyes.

"Emiko!" Mama called. "Your *friend* is here."

Emiko, never *Amy*, as my friends at school call me.

"Coming!" I gathered[3] up a small red purse and glanced[3] once again in the mirror. The flowered sarong exposed my shoulders and clung to me so that I seemed taller and even more slender[3] than I was. Did I look "too" Oriental tonight?

But, wasn't that what Adam liked?

Lifting the ginger lei from its box, I lowered it carefully over my head. Adam had sent it. I closed my eyes and breathed in its rich fragrance[3], smiling. The flowers had come with his note: To my exotic, inscrutable Amy ...

Reading it for the tenth time I felt the same rush of pleasure.[1] And doubt. Pleasure that he'd singled me out.[1] And doubt as to why exactly. Oh, yes, I was bright and popular and even pretty in my way. But so were a lot of other girls. It was my differentness that intrigued[3] him, my quietness, for I often kept thoughts to myself. In truth, I was a puzzle to him and a novelty. He hadn't come to realize yet that I live in two very different worlds – the world of today at school and with him – the world of yesterday at home with my parents. Sometimes even I wasn't sure where I truly belonged.

The mumble[4] of voices downstairs reminded me that Adam would be trying to make small talk with Mama and Papa, which wouldn't be easy. Even though they meant to be polite, my parents had a way of

2 **to leap** to jump suddenly from place to place – 3 **luau** [luːˈaʊ] an Hawaiian feast – 8 **almond** [ˈɑːmənd] *Mandel* – 12 **sarong** [səˈrɒŋ] long cloth worn around the waist or under the arms as a skirt, especially in Malaysia and Indonesia – **to expose** to allow to see, to make visible – 13 **to cling, clung, clung to s.o./s.th.** *here:* to be tight around s.o./s.th.– 16 **ginger** [ˈdʒɪndʒə] tropical flower of Asia *(Ingwer)* – **lei** [leɪ] *(Hawaiian)* garland of flowers worn around the neck – 19 **inscrutable** difficult to understand, mysterious – 25 **novelty** something new

making strangers feel uncomfortable, closing the shutters[1] behind their eyes.

I hurried down the stairs, glimpsing[3] Adam before he saw me. Seated in a straight-backed chair opposite my parents, he leaned forward, chatting[3] in that easy way that seems too natural to him.

He turned just as I reached the last step, and seeing me, jumped up. "Amy!" He seemed to draw in his breath as he reached me and held out a hand. "You look – wonderful!"

"Thanks," I said softly, and the butterflies began swarming[2] again. Adam did that to me, took my breath away, turned me shy. Wearing white chinos and a blue shirt the color of his eyes, he seemed to glow. When I'd first seen him I'd almost stopped breathing. To me he was beautiful – tall, built like statues I'd seen of young Greeks. I smiled to myself at the thought that my fingers had ruffled[3] that head of golden hair, had traced the strong jaw, that my lips had kissed his. Even at this moment his fingers, entwined[3] in mine, sent electric charges[3] through me.

"Emiko, you will not be home late," Mama said.

I'd forgotten my parents in the excitement and now turned in surprise to them. "The dance ends at one, Mama."

"Some of the kids will be going out afterward for coffee and pizza, Mrs. Sumoto," Adam said.

"You will be home as soon as the dance is over, Emiko," Papa said.

Adam's hand tightened in mine. I hesitated only an instant, swallowing disappointment, then said, "Yes, Papa." The flatness[1] of my father's statement left no room for discussion.

"Well, good night, Mr. and Mrs. Sumoto," Adam said. "We'll be home right after the dance. Thanks for lending me your beautiful daughter."

Mama smiled and her face softened. "Have a good time and drive carefully." The door closed behind us but not before I glimpsed Papa's face, so unbending[1] and stubborn that it took some of the joy of the evening away.

As Adam eased[3] the car out into the road I wondered if he ever noticed where I lived. Ours was a modest neighborhood of middle-class

7 **to draw in one's breath** to breathe deeply because of a surprise – 11 **chinos** ['tʃi:nəʊz] trousers made of the same cotton material as used for jeans – **to glow** to shine brightly – 15 **to trace** *here:* to move along the edge of s.th. – **jaw** bone in which the teeth are set – 24 **to swallow** *here:* to accept, not to protest – 32 **stubborn** refusing to change one's opinion – 35 **modest** not very rich

homes built in the fifties. A pleasant block of neatly[3] kept lawns and crepe-myrtle trees at the curb. We were one of two Japanese families in the block, along with a black and a Latino family; the rest were *hakujin* – white. I would never have given this any thought were it not for the knowledge of where Adam lived. The homes on Valley Vista were huge, with fourteen or more rooms and land around them so that you couldn't hear the neighbor's television or his dog barking. When I first saw his home I thought of a castle on a hill away from the noise, the worries, the poverty, and the crowds.

As far as I knew only white people lived on the Vista. Early each weekday morning buses lumbered[3] up the hill to unload the cleaning ladies who scattered[3] through the streets and disappeared into the houses. During the day the only nonwhites likely to be seen were the gardeners, Latinos and Asians and blacks. Then, late in the afternoon, the doors of the big houses opened again and the cleaning ladies spilled[3] out, making their tired way back to the buses, back down the hills to their own neighborhoods.

"I'm sorry about the curfew," I said, glancing anxiously at Adam's profile[2] in the darkness, and moved closer to him. "Maybe we can leave the dance a little early so we can have time alone together."

"Is he always so strict?"

"Only since Hideo married without his permission. Papa wanted him to marry a Japanese girl, but my brother was in love with Sue. The only thing he could do was what he did, marry her and then tell Papa." I folded[2] my hands tightly in my lap. "Papa worries that I'll do the same thing now. He's afraid he's losing control of the family."

"You'd think he'd be pleased, if she's a nice girl and makes Hideo happy."

"Yes, you'd think so. But Papa doesn't trust ... no, not that so much. It's that he's proud of who he is. And besides ..." I hesitated, not sure I knew Adam well enough yet to share the family history, the *shame* of the internment camps, and hoped he wouldn't ask me to go on. But we were close to the school now and his attention was taken

2 **crepe-myrtle** ['kreɪp 'mɜ:tl] a tree with colorful flowers found in warm climates – **curb** [kɜ:b] (*BE* kerb) edge of the sidewalk (pavement) – 3 **Latino** [læ'ti:nəʊ] person from Central or South America – 18 **curfew** ['kɜ:fju:] a certain time of the evening after which people (or some people) are not allowed to be away from home – 25 **lap** the upper part of the legs when one is seated – 31 **to share** *here:* to tell s.o. else about s.th. – 32 **internment camps** camps Japanese and Japanese-Americans were forced to live in during World War Two

by other cars arriving, by friends on motorcycles waving to us, by the search for a parking space.

We followed the tiki torches to the school courtyard,[3] where the lunch tables and chairs, which normally filled the space, were set up in a circle around a large wooden dance floor and band platform. "Oh, Adam … it's magical!" I exclaimed[2] at everything. Colored lights were strung high over the yard between buildings. They blinked[2] lazily in the warm, dry breeze.[2] The air felt like silk to my skin and the band played a sensual rhythm that made my hands want to talk and my body to sway.

Adam tightened an arm around my waist and moved me along. "Justin promised to come early and hold a table for the gang." He waved to one of the girls who always seemed to be watching for him.

"Wait, Adam," I said, tugging at his arm. "There's Carol and Juan. Let's stop and say hi." I used to see a lot of Carol before I began dating[3] Adam, and realized I missed her.

"Hi, guys," I greeted. "Carol, you look great!" She wore a full, fiesta-style skirt and white lace blouse which emphasized her satin-smooth olive skin.

Carol smiled and looked down at herself. "It's not quite a luau dress but it's the only thing close I've got. You look smashing,[3] Amy. Doesn't she, Juan?"

Juan growled appreciatively[1] and made a playful lunge at me.

"Down, fella, down!" Adam said, laughing. I stepped back, touched hands together, and bowed in traditional Oriental fashion.

"Hey, how about joining us? You can see we've got plenty of room." Juan indicated[2] the six empty seats at their table.

"Thanks, but no. We just stopped to say hi." Adam pressed my back. "Besides, Amy promised to teach me the hula." He held up a hand in parting.[2]

"See you in class Monday!" Carol called after us, and I waved back. Something about the way they looked – disappointed, subdued[3] –

3 **tiki** ['ti:kɪ] wooden image with decorations as used on the Pacific islands – **torch** *Fackel* – 7 **to string, strung, strung** to put together on a thread – 8 **silk** *Seide* – 9 **sensual** giving physical pleasure – 10 **to sway** to swing from side to side – 11 **waist** the part of the body between the ribs and the hips – 14 **to tug** to pull hard at s.th. – 18 **lace** *Spitze* – **satin** ['sætɪn] cloth that is soft and shiny – 23 **to growl** to make an angry sound like a dog – **lunge** sudden forward movement – 24 **Down fella, down!** fella = fellow; usually said to a dog that has become too excited – 25 **to bow** [baʊ] to bend the body down as a sign of respect – **fashion** *here:* manner – 29 **hula** dance typical of the Pacific islands – 32 **subdued** [səb'dju:d]

made me wonder why I hadn't thought to ask *them* to join us. Would Adam have minded? Or was it because I had my own misgivings? Being the only nonwhite in his crowd, I didn't always feel entirely comfortable. Sometimes I swallowed things I wanted to say, like at home where I couldn't always speak my mind[3] and where Papa's word was law.

I thought of the day I'd told Adam's friends about how Juan had chased me around the fountain,[2] picked me up, and thrown me in. Most of the gang laughed, but a few of them got strange, condescending looks on their faces, which made me sorry I'd spoken. Sometimes I wondered if Adam's friends really liked me, or if they accepted me only because I was his girl.

"Come on, you guys!" Adam said in greeting as soon as we reached the table Justin had saved. "On your feet. Everybody, up up! Amy's gonna teach us the hula."

"Adam," I cried. "They probably already know how!"

"Those klutzes? Unlikely."

The good-natured responses[2] and jokes that followed while each of the couples made its way to the dance floor made me a little less uncomfortable. But as I began to demonstrate how to stand, how to move the hips and slide the feet, and especially how to use the hands, a little crowd gathered.

"Do it, Amy! Come on, show us!" someone cried as the band started a hula. A chant[2] went up, echoing[2] the idea.

"Her grandmother lived in Hawaii," Adam told everyone with a voice full of pride. "Go to it, Amy! Show 'em!"

Slowly, I let the music take over my body. In moments I forgot where I was and who was watching. I danced for Adam, swaying my hips in languid movements while my hands and fingers spoke of raindrops falling and wind blowing ripples on the sea, and of two people very much in love. All the time I danced my eyes stayed locked[1] on Adam's and told him of feelings I'd never put into words.

Applause[2] broke my trance. I looked about in embarrassment,[1] then covered my face with my hands and rushed off the floor.

Adam followed. "Hey, honey,[3]" he said, gathering[3] me into his

2 **misgivings** feelings of doubt or fear – 9 **condescending** showing that one is better than others – 15 **gonna** *(AE informal)* going to – 17 **klutz** [klʌts] *(Yiddish)* foolish or clumsy person – 21 **hip** part of the body between the upper thigh and the waist – 26 **Go to it!** Start! – 29 **languid** ['læŋgwɪd] *here:* slow and sensual – 30 **ripple** small wave – 33 **trance** sleep-like state

arms. "What's this? You were beautiful! I'll never forget it. Every guy here wants to dance with you. I think I'll sell chances."

I giggled into his chest then looked up to see the amusement[2] in his eyes. "What did I tell you? Here comes Justin with that determined look."

I didn't quite like Justin, though I'd never told Adam that. Everything about him was big. His height and girth, but especially his mouth. Even so I distrusted[1] my judgment because the jokes he often told didn't seem to offend[3] anyone except me.

Justin bowed low in a sweeping[3] movement. "Will the lovely Princess Amy do me the honor?"

"Humor him, honey, but only one dance. Who knows, with your charm,[2] maybe you'll change this ugly gorilla into a handsome[3] prince."

I wished Adam hadn't accepted for me, but I followed Justin to the dance floor, his moist hand gripping mine. I forced a smile as we began to dance, unable to think of a thing to say.

"So I told them," Justin bellowed, "if they had just let me get the band they wouldn't have had that kind of trouble."

"That's true, Justin."

"... and you should have seen the pass. Fifty yards!"

"That's great, Justin." All I had to do was offer an occasional approving sound and Justin would keep going. It was a relief when Juan appeared, working his way through the dancers. He tapped[3] Justin on the shoulder. "Mind if I cut in[3]?"

Justin swung around. "Sure do, enchilada. Buzz off!"

Juan's grin[2] froze and I was afraid he'd start a fight. "Okay, *gabacho,*" he said lightly, "we'll let Amy decide."

"You heard me. Buzz off!"

"Wait!" I stepped between them and put a hand out to each to keep them apart. "Justin, please, I promised Juan yesterday that I'd save a

2 **chances** *(AE)* tickets in a lottery (the winner being allowed to dance with Amy) – 3 **to giggle** [g] to laugh quietly in a silly way – 4 **determined** firmly decided – 7 **girth** the distance around s.o.'s waist – 12 **to humor s.o.** (*BE* humour) to keep s.o. happy by agreeing to this person's wishes – 16 **moist** slightly wet – 18 **to bellow** to shout in a deep voice – 21 **pass** *(football)* act of passing the ball to another player – 22 **to approve** to show and say that s.th. is right – 23 **relief** feeling glad because s.th. unpleasant has not happened – 26 **enchilada** [ˌentʃɪˈlɑːdə] Mexican dish made with meat and chili sauce; *here:* derogatory word for a Mexican-American – **Buzz off!** *(slang)* Go away! – 27 **gabacho** [gəˈbɒtʃəʊ] *(derog.)* Mexican-American word for a white American

dance. You understand." Before he could answer I took Juan's arm and steered[3] him away.

"That bastard[2]!" Juan cried, resisting[2] me. "I'm tired of his snide remarks. I swear[2], next time he comes near me I'll beat his brains out."

"Juan, please," I cried. "You should know him by now. He's about as sensitive as a blob."

"That bigot! How do you stand the guy, Amy? How can you have anything to do with him?"

"I don't! It's Adam I'm going with."

"They're all that way, those rich white dudes! Scratch the surface and there's a Justin inside every one of them."

"Now who's being bigoted? Adam's not like that and you know it! Juan, please, you're spoiling[3] the whole evening. Let's forget it."

"You don't like making waves, do you, Amy? When are you going to take a stand?" The music ended and we faced[1] each other. "Are you one of them, or one of us? Do you know who you are and will you stand up for it[3], or are you gonna let everyone else call your shots?"

"That's not fair! It's not a war. I don't have to choose sides. I like everyone!"

"Well, *good luck!* If you ever take off your blinders you might be interesting." Juan stalked[3] off just as Adam was arriving.

"I'm going to have a talk with that guy," Adam said when I told him about Justin's rudeness. "He's really getting out of hand[3] lately. But Juan's got a chip on his shoulder, too. We're not all Justins."

"I know," I said, smiling at Adam. "He doesn't know the first thing about the kind of person you are."

"Which is?"

"Are you fishing for compliments?"

"Never. Which is?"

"Loyal, honest, kind, generous ..." I counted each one off on my fingers.

3 **snide** meant to hurt people's feelings – 6 **sensitive** understanding the feelings of other people – **blob** s.th. small without shape – 7 **bigot** ['bɪgət] person who is very intolerant of other ideas, religions, races, etc. – 10 **dude** [du:d] *(AE slang)* person – 15 **to take a stand** to firmly express an opinion about s.th. – 17 **to call the shots** *(AE)* to be in control of a situation – 21 **blinders** s.th. a horse wears to restrict its vision so that it is not frightened by traffic – 24 **rudeness** impolite behavior – 25 **to have a chip on one's shoulder** to quarrel because one thinks one is being treated unfairly – 29 **to fish for compliments** to try to make s.o. say s.th. admirable about oneself – 31 **generous** ['dʒenərəs] ready to give freely

At last Adam laughed. "You forgot sexy."

The band started a slow number and Adam put his arms around me. When we were together like this I knew there were no differences between us, none at all. We were perfect for each other.

Chapter 2

Light from a passing car brought me back to reality. “Adam! What time is it?”

I struggled out of his embrace and fumbled[2] for the keys in my bag. “Oh, no! It’s after two!”

Adam tried to bring me close again, but even the rapid[2] pounding[4] of his heart against mine didn’t quiet that flutter of fear. Papa had said, “Right after the dance.” That meant one o’clock, or minutes after. Where had the time gone? How had I let this happen?

“Stop worrying,” Adam said. “They’re probably fast asleep. Just another minute.”

“No, no, please!” I yanked away, found the front door key, and, trembling, pushed it into the lock. Hardly looking back, I whispered, “Good night. See you tomorrow.” And then I closed the door as quietly as possible.

For a moment I stood still adjusting[3] to the darkness of the entry hall, wondering if I could get up the stairs to my room without the steps creaking[4], without my parents knowing. I wanted to fall into bed, close my eyes, and think about Adam.

“Emiko?”

I swung around at my father’s voice coming from the kitchen in the back. They were up, waiting. My mouth went dry and fear tingled[3] all through me. “Yes, Papa?”

“Come in here.”

Clutching my purse so the clasp hurt my hand, I crossed the hall and opened the door to the kitchen. Mama and Papa were seated at the table, a pot of tea between them. Papa’s sallow skin had taken on a gray look and the lines in the weathered[1] cheeks ran deeper than I remembered. His clasped hands were cracked[1] and rough from the print shop he owns and runs.

Mama worked in Uncle’s fish store every day. I smelled the lemon-scented soap she used to cover the smell of handling fish.

“It’s after two,” Papa announced, dark eyes fixed accusingly on me.

3 **embrace** act of putting one’s arms around s.o. as a sign of love – 11 **to yank** to pull suddenly – 24 **to clutch** to hold tightly – **purse** *(AE)* woman’s handbag – **clasp** metal part that keeps the opening of a handbag closed – 26 **sallow** yellowish – 27 **cheek** side of the face below the eye – 28 **clasped** held tightly together – 29 **print shop** *Druckerei* – 30 **lemon-scented** ['sentɪd] with the smell of lemon

My glance went to the yellow kitchen clock on the wall behind him. I'd bought it for my parents' last anniversary.[2] "I know, Papa. I'm sorry."

"You were to be home by one, no later."

"Yes, Papa. I'm sorry."

"It's not enough to be sorry! A girl should obey[3] her parents."

I bowed my head, wanting to scream, *I'm seventeen! What parents stay up until two o'clock on a Saturday night waiting for their grown daughter to come home?* Didn't Papa know this was the twentieth century, that this was America, not Japan?

"This would never have happened if you had been out with a Japanese boy," Papa went on. "A Japanese boy would have had proper respect. He would have had you home on time!"

"Adam respects me, Papa. Please don't say that." It was so hard to speak politely and not cry.

"You've only known him three months," Mama said, her face as set and ungiving as Papa's. "Three months is no time at all. What does anyone know of another in so short a time? A girl does not show respect for herself to stay out till all hours with a boy she hardly knows."

I clutched the purse harder and looked away. No one could argue or disagree with Mama or Papa. It was just not done. If I dared ask a reason for some order, Papa would merely say, "Because I said so."

"He is not like us. They are all the same, these *hakujin.* I work with them every day." Papa's voice rose in imitation of one of the rich housewives who came into his shop regularly to have their club news printed. "'How is your family, Mr. Sumoto? Your wife? Your college son? Your daughter?' After all this time, do they remember Hideo's name, or yours? No! And when I answer, their minds are elsewhere, wishing I would hurry."

"Adam isn't like that!"

"He is. He's one of them. And don't forget it. He's not one of our people, which should be reason enough. And he is from money."

I wanted to scream, *Why must you put doubt in my head? Who cares if he's not Japanese? Who cares if his father makes more money than you do?* Instead, I said, "Papa, I'm sorry. Please forgive me. It was my fault. We were home by one and I should have come right in!"

"It doesn't matter whose fault." Papa pushed a hand against the

36 **fault** responsibility for having done s.th. wrong

small of his back and stood up. “You will not see this boy so often; it is not good.”

“But tomorrow ... today ... we’re going to the beach.”

“No,” Papa said. “You are not. You will not see him for a week. You will come home right after school each day and do your homework and any other work Mama needs of you. Today, you will come with us to visit Hideo.”

“Papa!” I cried in disbelief[1]. “Papa, that’s not fair!” My throat tightened and tears sprang to my eyes. They were treating me like a twelve-year-old.

Papa held up a hand. “You will do as I say, Emiko. It’s late. Now go to bed.”

I looked to my mother, hoping for support, but Mama kept her back turned as she rinsed the dishes and put them in the drainer.

A strange strangled cry came out of my throat and I turned swiftly to hide my feelings.

“Good night, Emiko,” Papa said.

“Good night, Mama, Papa,” I whispered, hurrying from the kitchen. I stumbled[3] through the dark hall and up the stairs to my room. Trembling, I threw myself on the bed and burst into tears.

I’d never phoned Adam at his home. My parents wouldn’t approve. I waited until Mama went out to the garden to pick the last of the summer squash and Papa was in the garage, working on his truck. And then I went to the phone with an ache in my stomach. If I couldn’t see Adam for a whole week, every day would be bleak and meaningless. What was I without him? And would I lose him?

I dialed hesitantly[1], then hung up. But if I didn’t call, Papa would be there when Adam arrived and *he* would tell Adam. That would be even worse. I reached for the phone again and took my hand away again. What if *his* mother answered?

At last I dialed the number and, heart thumping[3], waited for someone to answer.

“Hello?”

1 **the small of one’s back** the part of the back that curves inwards – 14 **to rinse** to remove the soap with fresh water – **drainer** s.th. that holds dishes to let them drip and dry – 15 **strangled** as if the throat had been pressed so as to make breathing difficult – 21 **to approve** [ə'pru:v] to consider an opinion or type of behavior to be good – 23 **squash** *(AE)* a vegetable similar to a pumpkin – *25* **bleak** cold and cheerless

"Hello. May I speak with Adam, please?" My voice sounded so low and timid, I had to repeat myself.

"Just a moment." In the background Adam's mother called, "Phone, Adam!"

"Who is it?"

"Some girl. I wish they'd stop calling here so often!"

Some girl. I felt suffocated with shame and doubt. Did girls call Adam often? Was I just one more girl to him? Until I heard his footsteps I stared blindly out the window to the garden. Mama looked so much at peace, bending among the rows of late-summer vegetables. If only I could feel like that.

"Hello?"

"Adam, it's me, Amy." I added my name in case he was expecting someone else.

"Hello, beautiful! Say, what's wrong?"

I spilled out[3] the whole unjust story from beginning to end. Biting my lip to keep back the pain, I finished with the final injustice[1]. "Papa grounded me for a week!"

"Amy, no! Didn't you tell him he's living in the Dark Ages? They check on you like the KGB! My parents are no angels, but they wouldn't ground me for a thing like that! They know I'm responsible. So are you! Why don't your parents see that?"

"You don't understand. It's a question of respecting your elders. It's – "

"They're always talking about respect. Where's their respect for you? I think your father just uses that word to keep you under his thumb!"

Maybe Adam was right. Maybe I should stand up to Papa more. Maybe I should be like other girls who shout at their parents to get their way. But that's not how I'd been brought up. Mama and Papa never raised their voices in anger at home, so how could I? Besides, Mama and Papa really meant well; they were good people.

"Parents!" Adam exclaimed with disgust. "Sometimes I wonder how either of us could have escaped all their prejudices. I think it's more than just coming home late that's bothering your father. It's me.

2 **timid** afraid, lacking courage – 7 **suffocated** as if not able to breathe properly – 18 **to ground s.o.**. *(AE) here:* to tell a child to stay at home as punishment – 19 **Dark Ages** period of history after the fall of Rome (476 AD) to 1000 AD; a time of little education and culture – 20 **KGB** secret police of the Soviet Union – 26 **to keep s.o. under one's thumb** [θʌm] to keep s.o. completely under one's control – 35 **to bother** ['bɒðə] to trouble

It's my not being Japanese! And my parents are just as bad. Their friends are as alike as slices of white bread. They distrust[1] anyone who isn't just like them. You remember how they wanted me to go to Westridge instead of Center High?"

"Oh, Adam ..."

Adam's anger seemed to melt at my sympathy. "That's why I care so much about you, Amy. You're not exactly like everyone I've ever known. You're you, and for the first time in my life I've chosen someone *I* like, not someone my parents picked out for me!"

My heart sang at his words and I curled into the phone, smiling.

"Listen," he said. "Don't worry about missing the beach party. We'll go another time if the weather stays good."

A vision of bikini-clad[3] girls with blond hair and blue eyes flashed through my head. "Will you go anyway?"

"Justin and Melissa expect me to pick them up."

"Oh."

"Don't worry, Amy. We'll see each other at school; after all, there's Otero's class. He's starting that Color Game thing we signed on for, remember? And we'll eat lunch together and" – he lowered his voice – "I'll walk you to classes even if I'm late for my own, because I can't stand the thought of not being close to you for a whole week." His voice grew husky.

Reassured, I closed my eyes, sharing a good silence, like an embrace. Then I glanced out the window. Papa had come out of the garage and was talking to Mama, wiping his hands on a big cloth that hung from his belt. Mama nodded, then lifted the heavy basket full of vegetables, and the two of them started back to the house.

"My parents are coming in. I've got to go, Adam. We're having dinner with Hideo and Sue. It's going to be strained and awful, but I have to go. I wish I could be with you instead."

"Don't worry, honey. Nobody's going to stop us from seeing each other. Right?"

"Right," I echoed, though I wasn't so sure. Until recently I hadn't thought how Adam's parents might feel about his dating me. But the last time I'd been to his house to tutor[2] his sister Bettina, I'd got an

4 **Westridge** name of a private school – **Center High** i.e. Center High School, a public (i.e. state)school – 10 **I curled into the phone** I held the telephone very close to me – 18 **to sign on for s.th.** to agree to take part in s.th: by signing one's name – 22 **husky** low and dry, as if having a sore throat – 23 **to reassure** to make free from fear, worry, or doubts – 29 **strained** full of tension or anxiety

inkling. Mrs. Tarcher knew Adam was seeing me. She smiled politely enough and said all the things, sort of. But I felt as if I was being tolerated, that it was only because I'd won the math contest and could help Bettina that she even talked to me. I couldn't shake the sense that she considered me "hired help."

"Bye, then, Amy, sweets. See you Monday."

"Bye. Have fun at the beach."

"Without you, no way."

The butterflies began swarming again. I hung up the phone, full of joy, and hurried into the kitchen before my parents came into the house. Mama would expect me to help wash the vegetables to bring to Hideo and Sue.

Hideo and Sue had rented a one-bedroom apartment in a small court and furnished it with things they'd bought at swap meets and through ads in the newspaper. Although the building was old and the paint so thick at the sills that windows didn't close properly, I liked it. An avocado[2] tree shaded their front door and they could sit outside on hot evenings on a small green lawn.

Papa had not seen Hideo for nearly a year because Hideo had married without his consent[3]. He had forbidden Mama and me to see him as well. I'd disobeyed once, but felt so guilty and afraid of being found out that I never went again.

It was only recently that they'd built a small bridge between them. This would be only the second time we'd visited. The first time had been frightfully awkward with long silences. I'd tried to help by exclaiming over everything. "Look, Papa, Mama, at the wonderful things Sue and Hideo have done!" Sue had bought a Japanese lantern[2] which Hideo had hung over the naked light bulb in the kitchen. Together they had stripped an old, ugly dresser and refinished it so the original, rich-grained wood showed through.

The first thing I did when I saw Sue was hug her, wishing mother could find it in her heart to do the same. But Mama merely smiled that

1 **inkling** hint, feeling – 5 **hired help** person paid to do some kind of task – 8 **no way** *(AE)* impossible – 13 **court** courtyard – 14 **to furnish** to put in furniture – **swap** [swɒp] **meet** *(AE)* when people get together to exchange things – 16 **sill** windowsill, board at the bottom of a window – 25 **to exclaim over s.th.** to speak about s.th. with strong feeling – 29 **to strip** to remove the paint – **dresser** *(AE)* chest of drawers *(BE)* – **to refinish** to give a new surface to furniture – 30 **rich-grained** with an attractive wood pattern – 31 **to hug s.o.** to hold s.o. tightly in your arms

fixed[2] polite smile she used for strangers and put the vegetables on the kitchen counter. "It smells marvelous, Sue, whatever it is!" I said, watching Mama.

"Chicken cacciatore." Sue looked over my shoulder at Mama. "I hope you like it. It's from the international cookbook Amy brought us."

"I like chicken," Mama said. "May I help put these vegetables away?"

"Oh, Mama Sumoto, would you?" Sue exclaimed overbrightly. "The fridge is kind of crowded, but maybe you can make room." She lifted the lid from a big iron pot and poked[3] at the chicken with a fork. Steam escaped into the kitchen, rich and sweet.

"Should I set the table, Sue?"

The visit was going well, I thought, carrying the card table into the living room and bringing in chairs. Hideo was showing Papa all the new things they'd bought or found, the travel posters on the wall, books and records, the large fern[2] that Sue had nursed[1] back to health by following Papa's instructions. I felt hopeful that this time Papa might actually look directly at Sue when she spoke and that Mama wouldn't just sit, hands folded, smiling.

"Isn't it wonderful what Hideo did with those bookshelves, Papa Sumoto?" Sue asked when we all sat down to dinner. Her pale face lit up into a brilliant[2] smile as she placed a hand on Hideo's strong, tanned arm.

"I think this is the time for me to go bring in the chicken!" Hideo said, laughing. He touched Sue's curly blond hair lovingly. "This woman is going to make my head swell[2] if I don't watch out."

"Never mind! I'd never have thought of using old bricks like that, would you, Mr. Sumoto ... Papa?"

Papa didn't answer. His eyes followed Hideo as he left the room. He'd be thinking that Sue should be in the kitchen not Hideo – that serving dinner was woman's work. I couldn't recall ever seeing Papa lift a finger to help in the kitchen.

"How's kindergarten?" I asked Sue, hoping she wouldn't notice Papa's rudeness. "Is it harder than teaching second grade?"

Eyes sparkling[3], she said. "Those little ones are just darling. They're

4 **chicken cacciatore** [kætʃə'tɔ:rə] an Italian dish made with chicken and tomato sauce – 10 **kind of** rather – 14 **card table** small table that can be folded – 23 **to light (lit, lit) up** to become bright – 24 **tanned** [tænd] brown because of sunlight – 26 **curly** ['kɜ:lɪ] wavy – 28 **brick** rectangular block of baked clay used for building walls – 35 **rudeness** impolite behavior – **grade** *(AE)* form *(BE)*

so tiny, you just want to wrap[3] them in your arms. But it's really hard. I have to be on my toes every second. They don't sit still very long yet." She lifted the salad bowl and offered it to me.

"She's just being modest," Hideo called from the kitchen. "Keeps those kids in line like a Marine sergeant!" In a moment he was back wearing oven mitts and carrying the steaming chicken casserole[2]. He lowered the pot to a wobbly snack tray and began ladling[3] out the contents.

A silence fell at the table.

"Papa?" I said at last. "We're going to do something very interesting in social studies Monday. It's a game. The kids get to wear color armbands which represent different social classes. They have to wear the bands twenty-four hours a day for the next four weeks! It's supposed to teach us what it's like to be rich or poor or in-between, and to be black or Latino ... or some other color."

Papa chewed carefully, then said. "You're Japanese; you already know what color you are."

"I think it sounds interesting, Amy," Sue said, exchanging glances with Hideo. "Lots of people have prejudices against others just because they're poor, or black or brown, or even ..." She stopped and I wondered if she was about to say "white." "If people had the chance to 'walk in the moccasins'[2] of someone else, maybe they'd understand and be more sympathetic."

"Papa, what do you think?" Hideo asked.

"I think it's a silly way to teach. Students should be reading books and doing homework, not playing games."

"Oh, Papa!" Hideo exclaimed, shaking his head in disbelief. "You never change!" His smile was loving. "But what do you think of the idea? Don't you think if we were all color-blind we'd get along better together? Come on, Papa, don't you?"

Papa sat straighter. "The day people don't judge others by their color is a day I never expect to see. That's just the way it is."

"Not everyone is that way, Papa," I said. *Adam, for one,* I thought, and it made me smile.

2 **to be on your toes** to be watchful and ready to act – 4 **modest** ['mɒdɪst] not showing off one's abilities, not proud – 5 **Marine sergeant** [mə'riːn 'sɑːdʒənt] a member of the United States Marine Corps, which is known for its hard training – 6 **oven** ['ʌvn] **mitts** kind of gloves used in the kitchen when handling hot objects – 7 **wobbly** unsteady, not stable – 11 **social studies** subject dealing with the history, government, and geography of a country – 16 **to chew** [tʃuː] to use one's teeth to make food in one's mouth smaller

"*We* don't judge others by their skin," Hideo said. "And we expect our children to be the same way." He turned to Sue. "Tell them, honey."

Sue reminded me of a trusting fawn as she gazed first at Papa, then at Mama, then Hideo, and finally me. "We're going to have a baby. I'm pregnant."

"Oh, Sue!" I jumped up and hugged her. "How wonderful Hideo!" I kissed my brother's cheek. "Isn't that tremendous![3] When?"

"May, I think."

"Mama, Papa! Say something," Hideo begged[3]. "Aren't you glad for us? You'll have a grandchild!"

Mama stretched a tentative hand across the table to touch Sue. Papa's face showed uncertainty. Had he hoped that Hideo's marriage wouldn't work? I ached[1] for my brother and Sue. They wanted Papa's approval[3] and blessing so badly. It would do so much to heal[3] the break they had created by marrying. But if Papa kept up this stubborn reserve[2], he'd lose them. They'd turn to each other for strength and support and the Sumoto family would be split[3] for good. I twisted the napkin in my lap tightly around my fingers, eyes on Papa.

"If you have a child now," he said, "your wife will have to stop working. How can you afford that?"

Hideo moved closer to Sue and put a protective arm around her shoulder. His voice turned cold. "My *wife's* name is Sue, Papa. I'd like to hear you call her that. And as for whether we can afford it or not, we'll manage. That's not your worry."

"My family is always my worry," Papa said. He cleared his throat and grunted as he always did when he felt uneasy, and looked at Mama. Finally, after what seemed a terribly long silence, he smiled fleetingly at Sue. "That would be nice, a baby, a child. A new Sumoto." He cleared his throat again and this time looked at Hideo. "That would be very nice. Yes. That is good news. ..." He paused for a long moment, and I wondered if he would finally say Sue's name, but his eyes slid[3] over her quickly and returned to his food.

4 **fawn** [fɔːn] a young deer less than a year old – 12 **tentative** uncertain – 15 **blessing** *Segen* – 18 **for good** for ever, always after that – **to twist** to change the shape of s.th. by turning tightly – 26 **to clear one's throat** to cough slightly in order to make it easier to speak – 27 **to grunt** to make a low rough sound, especially when irritated

Chapter 3

From the moment I joined Adam the next day I felt uneasy and deceitful. It was as if Papa were standing just behind me, watching. Of course that was ridiculous; he was at work thinking of other things, yet I couldn't shake the sense that I was doing wrong. Papa had intended I not see Adam *at all,* and that meant anyplace, not at school or after. And here we were talking, pretending Papa wouldn't mind.

"I'm beginning to feel as if I'm Romeo and you're Juliet," Adam joked as we stood apart from the other students for the few minutes before the bell rang. "My mother's not too crazy about us, either."

"How do you know? Did she say something?"

Adam squeezed my shoulders reassuringly[1]. "Now, don't start worrying. You have to know my mother. She's just funny about some things. Won't come right out and say what she thinks, but comes at it through the back door. 'Have you seen that Conley girl lately, dear? Such a lovely young woman.' That's Mom." Adam made a face. "Eileen Conley's a spoiled brat, about as nice as a spider. When I told Mom that, you can guess she wasn't too pleased."

"I suppose we'll survive," I said. "Papa said one week, so maybe it won't be too awful. Except ..."

"Except what?"

"What if we choose different colors in Mr. Otero's class?" I looked aside as the first period bell rang. "Will it mean we're not supposed to talk to each other?"

"Don't even *think* such a terrible thing!" Adam took my arm and we began pushing through the crowd into the building. "Listen, Amy. Nobody can keep us apart. Not your father, my mother, Otero, or his entire so-called police force. Nobody." He stepped aside to let me pass. "It's entirely up to us and how *we* feel about each other, right?"

"Right," I echoed, wanting to believe him, but my stomach churned[3] with uncertainty. It had seemed a fun idea, taking Otero's social studies elective together because of his "Color Game." I'd heard about the game from others who'd taken the class before, heard

1 **deceitful** [dɪ'si:tfʊl] dishonest – 3 **ridiculous** [rɪ'dɪkjʊləs] absurd – 13 **to come right out** not to hesitate, to be direct – 16 **spoiled brat** a child with a bad character because it has always been allowed to do what it wants – **spider** *Spinne* – 22 **period** (*AE*) lesson (*BE*) – 27 **entire** whole, complete – **police force** *Polizeitruppe* – 31 **elective** a course or subject that can be chosen, i.e. that one does not have to take

enough to think it might be more than just interesting. It might be important to Adam and me in some way, might prove if our relationship really had a future. I hadn't considered when I teased Adam into signing up with me that the game might also separate us for the next umpteen weeks. Would our feelings for each other survive?

Trying to ignore those fears, I climbed the stairs to the second-floor class with Adam three periods later. As we hurried down the hall I saw the cluster[3] of kids waiting outside the social studies room because Otero was late. There were the usual groupings – black kids off to one side, a small circle of Latino kids, and nearest the room the white kids, with Justin in their midst[2], getting laughs. Several students were hanging around who weren't in the class; the G4 police force, I wondered?

Otero catapulted[2] from a room across the hall, shaking out a clump[3] of keys. He unlocked the classroom door and everyone started pouring[3] in. I took my usual seat with Adam beside me, near the front of the room. "Do you suppose where you sit means anything?" I asked, settling[3] my books under the chair. "Just look. You and I always sit where we can look Otero straight in the eye. Justin always sits right near the door so he can bolt[3] as soon as the bell rings."

"Yeah," Adam said. "And Paul Thomas always sits where Otero can't see him, kind of slouched down. So, what's it mean? For that matter, does the fact that Otero scurries[3] around like a squirrel whenever we see him mean anything?"

I liked Mr. Otero. Most kids did. It was because he seemed so really excited about what he taught. And from what I heard, he cared about the students, because you'd often find him staying late to talk. He was kind of funny, too. I liked how he joked about his baldness[3], saying what didn't grow on top grew twice as thick at his chin. And he sure had a knack of keeping my interest in class; fifty minutes went by like ten.

"Today," he said, coming around to the front of his desk, "we're going to begin a great social experiment. For the next four weeks we'll be playing what I call the Color Game. In just four weeks we're going to change the world." Otero began writing on the board as he spoke, turning from time to time back to the class. "Imagine you're on a new planet where colors represent special status," he said. "Blue is the

3 **to tease** *here:* to beg s.o. in an annoying way until that person does what you want– 5 **umpteen** (*informal*) many *(zig)* – 22 **slouched down** not sitting upright, sitting lazily – **for that matter** and by the way – 23 **squirrel** *Eichhörnchen* – 30 **knack** [næk] ability

highest color. Blues are superior[2] beings[3]. Think of purity[1], of blue bloods, those with money, respect, and prestige. Blue children attend private schools and go to the best colleges. Their parents travel without worrying about cost; they live the good life in beautiful homes with maids and gardeners. And they intend to keep it that way." Otero stood aside so the class could read what he'd written on the board. I copied it into my notebook: Blue = upper class.

"Now, below the Blues are the Dark Greens. Like the upper middle class on earth. Dark Green people are often workaholics[1]. They figure[3] if they try a little harder they'll make it[3] to the Blues. Dark Green children almost always finish college. They're expected by their parents to go into the family business or become important in their professions. They're aware of the colors below them, the Light Greens and Oranges. But they're too busy trying to keep what they have and do even better to consider lending these less fortunate colors a hand."

What is my family? I wondered uneasily. *Dark Green? No, not quite. Aspiring to be.* Adam, of course was a Blue.

"Now, below the Dark Greens you'll find the Light Greens. They are the most numerous in society – the blue-collar workers, the lower middle class. Light Greens don't have it easy. If they have a job and a decent place to live where crime isn't too terrible, they're grateful. Their kids may go to junior college; few graduate. Light Greens aspire to become Dark Greens, but many are happy just to keep their heads above water."

Otero chuckled[3] with a kind of delighted satisfaction. "Finally we come to the Oranges. Now, there's a sad group. They're often out of work, on welfare, in trouble with the law, and no matter how hard they work, if indeed they can get jobs, they can barely make ends meet. Since welfare breeds welfare, you find second- and third-generation Oranges with big families and often no father figure around.

"Oranges would like a bigger piece ... in fact any piece ... of the planet's apple pie, but the way society operates, they may never get it." He paused, then said, "Of course these are all the stereotypes[2] of our class system."

5 **maid** [meɪd] woman servant – 13 **to be aware of** to know about – 15 **to lend a hand** to help – 17 **to aspire** to want very much to achieve s.th. – 22 **junior college** (*AE*) an institution that offers a two-year course that is the same as the first two years of a college or university – 27 **on welfare** receiving help or money from the state because of being too poor – 28 **barely** only just – **to make ends meet** to earn just enough money for one's needs – 29 **to breed, bred, bred** to cause, to produce

Even though I'd written it down, I wasn't sure all the colors were sorted[2] out in my head yet. Pretty soon Otero would have us selecting a color. What did I want to be? Certainly not an Orange or Light Green. No. Who'd want to have to struggle so hard to get along? It would be fine to be a Dark Green or Blue. They had respect and money to live well. That's what I wanted.

"I hope you've got all the colors straight," Otero said, "because now I'm going to explain the rules of etiquette on this unique planet." He toyed[1] with a stick of chalk, then said, "We have a system of bowing in our new society. Oranges must always show their inferiority[3] by bowing when they meet their superiors, all colors above them. Light Greens must bow to the Dark Greens and Blues. Dark Greens bow to the Blues. But the Blues, bless them, don't bow to anyone. Why should they? They're top dogs[3]." He thought for a moment. "We have sex discrimination in our society, also, but we'll discuss that next time we meet. I wouldn't want to confuse you with too much at once. Especially you *Oranges.*"

I laughed, along with everyone else. It was easy laughing when you weren't the one looked down on, and I had no thought that I could possibly become an Orange.

"Any questions so far?"

I raised my hand. "What if you aren't the same color as a friend? Besides bowing, is there anything else you have to do?"

Otero glanced at Adam, and I blushed, sure he knew why I asked the question. "Inferior colors may *not* speak with or socialize[1] with superior colors. A superior color may address an inferior one, but not vice versa[3]. Understood?"

I reached an icy hand across the aisle to join with Adam's warm one and gave him a worried look.

"What's the penalty for disobedience?" Adam asked.

"You can be fined, harassed, given lower status, any of a number of things."

"That's okay." Adam grinned that warm, confident smile I loved so much. "We just won't let anyone know."

4 **to get along** to manage – 8 **etiquette** ['etıket] proper social behavior – 13 **bless them** *here:* expression of good wishes – 24 **to blush** to become red in the face – 28 **aisle** [aıl] passage between rows of seats – 30 **penalty** ['penltı] punishment – **disobedience** refusal to do what one is told – 31 **to fine** to punish s.o. by making this person pay a sum of money – **to harass** to trouble and annoy continuously – 33 **confident** showing or feeling a trust in one's own abilities

Otero grinned right back. "I wouldn't count on that, Tarcher. We've got a spy network you wouldn't believe. Anyone who ever took part in the Color Game before – maybe three hundred students – will be watching you. And then, of course there's the police force you'll meet in a moment, the G4's. In addition, you're encouraged to report[3] on each other if you see any rules broken. You get extra points for squeal–[3] er, uh ... reporting, and the more points you earn, the better chance to move up in society."

"Ah, come on, Mr. Otero," Adam said. "We don't go around squealing on each other in real life. Besides, we don't really have class differences. Look around. We're all friends here. I don't care how much money anybody's got, and I don't give a hoot[3] what color anyone is."

"Really? Tell me, Tarcher. When was the last time you had a black friend home to dinner, or a Latino? How many minority students sit at the same lunch table with you and your white friends?"

Adam's face turned a bright shade[3] of pink. "I have soccer friends to the house. ..." he protested, but I knew Otero had made a point.

"For that matter," the teacher continued, his attention back to the class, "how many of you black students have Latino or white friends? Friends, not acquaintances[3]? And how many of you Latinos have black friends?" Only a few hands went up. "I thought so. Well, that's what this class is all about. We're going to expose the prejudices many of us have and maybe build some bridges between us." He pulled at his beard and said, "Okay! Now to sum up before you meet the G4's. Good behavior counts. The students who earn the most game points get credits[2] toward a higher grade. Call it a prize. So, if you want a good grade in this class, play the game to win." He stepped back behind the desk. "Okay, G4's. Explain about the armbands and journals before we choose colors."

"Journals?"

"Right." Otero reached behind him for a small spiral[3] notebook, which he held up to the class. "You'll need something like this to keep a daily record of your feelings and experiences during the Color Game. If you don't keep it up to date, or don't have it with you wherever you are, you can get in trouble from a G4."

"Everywhere? I'm on the track team. Got no pockets in my shorts."

"Everywhere," Otero repeated. "Tie it to your back, if you have to!"

2 **spy** a person who watches others secretly *(Spion)* – 5 **to encourage** to give active support to s.o. – 22 **to expose** to make known, to uncover – 26 **grade** *(AE)* mark *(BE)* – 36 **track** *(AE)* athletics *(BE)*

Five students came to the front of the room. Otero said they'd all played the Color Game before and had volunteered to be G4's, the police force. "You can't put much over on them because they've been exactly where you are now," he explained. "They know just what you're thinking and feeling and what ways you may try to sabotage[2] the game. But they're also here as counselors. When things get too heavy and you need someone to sort things out with, they're here to help."

Police force. It sounded so formidable, but they stood there watching us and smiling.

Mary, one of the girl G4's, stepped forward. She wore a karate uniform that made her look sort of intimidating and official. She introduced each of the G4's by name and then said, "We can challenge you any time of day or night. Anyplace. Asking to see your armbands and journals. We keep records[3] on everyone, putting down what we observe and what others tell us about civil disobedience, uppityness to the higher classes, and so on."

"What's the penalty for assaulting a G4?" Juan called out, making everyone laugh.

"Death."

I giggled, beginning to relax. Nobody seemed to take the game very seriously. A few more questions were answered, then one of the G4's took a box and plastic bag from Otero.

"Now, this is how we go about choosing colors," Mary said. "In this bag we have a lot of disks[2], blue ones, dark green ones, light greens, and oranges." She held up the plastic bag and handed the box to another G4. "Since there are many more poor people than rich, there are more light greens and oranges than other colors.

"What you'll do is reach into the plastic bag, pick a disk, and show it to me. Jennifer will hand you an armband of the color you chose, and Brian will make a record of your color in our record book." She shook the disk bag vigorously. "Okay, who wants to go first?"

2 **to volunteer** to offer to do s.th. – 3 **you can't put much over on them** you can't fool or deceive them – 6 **counselor** ['kaʊnsələ] (*BE* counsellor) adviser – 7 **heavy** *here:* difficult – 9 **formidable** frightening, causing anxiety – 12 **intimidating** causing one to become frightened – 13 **to challenge** to stop s.o. and demand an answer to questions – 15 **to put down** *here:* to write down – 16 **civil disobedience** using non-violent ways to protest against an unfair law or system of government – **uppityness** behaving as if one were better or more important than one really has a right to be – 18 **to assault** [ə'sɔ:lt] to make a sudden and violent attack – 32 **vigorously** energetically

As students began reaching into the bag for their disks I turned to Adam. "What color would you like to be?"

"Light Green, I think. Then I'd get to see how the other half lives without having to be in abject poverty. How about you?"

"I'd like that, too." I didn't want to admit my real preference. After all, any color would be fine as long as Adam chose it, too.

In moments Mary was in front of me holding the bag out. "Oh, I don't like this!" I cried, backing off. "You go first, Adam."

"Pick!" Mary ordered. "You're holding us up[3]."

Her harsh tone startled me. I closed my eyes and reached into the bag, feeling around among the cold disks for the right one. If I concentrated hard enough, maybe I could influence my choice so I'd pick a light green. At last I grasped[3] a disk and slowly withdrew[3] it. "I can't even look! What is it?"

"Blue!" Adam announced, disappointed. "You're a Blue."

"Here's your band," Jennifer said. She helped me put it on. "Always wear it on your right arm so we can see it, and give your name and color to G4 Brian."

Secretly pleased, I tightened the Velcro, then held my arm out for Adam to see. "Now you! And please pick a blue!"

"I've got one chance in four, so who knows?" Adam plunged[3] his hand into the bag, dug[3] around a while, then brought out a disk.

"Orange!" I cried as he opened his fist[3]. "Oh, Adam, no!"

Adam's forehead wrinkled in uncertainty, but he took it all in good cheer[3]. "So, I'm an Orange. Bottom of the barrel. This should be interesting." He held out his arm for the color band. Jennifer contemptuously threw his band on the floor and turned away.

The G4's moved on, holding out the disk bag, handing out color bands and recording each student's choice, but all of a sudden Adam and I didn't have anything to say to each other. Just wearing the blue band and knowing what it stood for made me feel different, kind of important somehow. I don't know how or why, but with the orange band on Adam, he seemed quieter, less self-assured[2].

Otero's voice boomed out over the commotion.

"When you've got your bands, change seats. Blues get the superior

4 **abject** ['æbdʒekt] miserable – 10 **harsh** unpleasant, sharp – 19 **Velcro** (trademark) *Klettverschluss* – 24 **forehead** part of the face above the eyebrows – **to wrinkle** *here:* to tighten the muscles so that lines form – 25 **bottom of the barrel** *here:* the lowest social position – 26 **contemptuous** [kən'temptjʊəs] showing that s.o. is completely worthless – 34 **to boom** to make a deep hollow sound – **commotion** noisy and excited activity

seats up front. Dark Greens behind them, Light Greens behind them, and Oranges in the back. Tomorrow there'll be some further seat changes according to sex, but we haven't time to explain that now, so just seat yourselves by color."

Adam picked up his books and prepared to take a seat in the back. I put a hand on his.

"Gotta play the game right, honey. But don't worry. Maybe we can change to the same color later. You be bad and get demoted, and I'll be good and get promoted[3]. Never know. So long. See you after class."

I watched him weave through the disorder of students moving to different seats until he found a place in the back of the room with the Oranges. He waved to me, then turned to a girl beside him.

Paul Thomas settled in the seat Adam had left, a wide grin on his dark face. Once I'd joined him at a cafeteria table, not knowing only blacks sat there. I'd felt as welcome as a good bout of flu and never made that mistake again.

"Hi, Amy," he greeted. "Man, this game's gonna be fun. I'm gonna love lording[2] it over those poor Orange brothers; they always got it so good."

"Oh, come on, Paul," I chided. "You're not going to take advantage of anyone just because you're a Blue?"

"Wanna bet?" He laughed with villainous glee. "Just watch. Hey, girl!" he called out to Carol, who was a Dark Green. "You didn't bow proper. G4! You see that?"

Had the game been rigged? So many of the minority students seemed to have chosen the dark colors, the upper classes, while most of the white students including Justin and Adam were either Light Green or Orange. Before I could prove my suspicion, Otero began explaining about the game money, which equaled the points. Blues would get more, and so on down the line[3], with Oranges getting the least.

"Hey, no fair!" Juan called out.

"Who said life is fair? G4, mark that Light Green's name down. If he complains again, we'll fine him." Otero paused as the bell rang to

7 **gotta** *(AE informal)* you have got to – 8 **to demote** to lower the position of s.o. – 10 **to weave, wove, woven** to move along by continuously changing one's direction – 15 **bout** [baʊt] **of flu** attack of influenza *(Grippe)* – 20 **to chide** to speak angrily to s.o. for doing s.th. wrong – 22 **wanna** *(AE informal)* do you want to – **villainous** ['vɪlənəs] evil, threatening to do harm – **glee** joy – 25 **to rig** to pre-arrange the outcome of a game, event, etc.

end the period. "G4's will pass out the money. Stay in your seats until you get yours." He held up a hand as several students rose to leave. "You may as well start playing the game right now! None of you will leave before your superior colors do. Blues first, Oranges last. See you tomorrow."

Adam bolted[3] from his seat, ignoring[2] Otero's instructions just as Brian handed me a wad[3] of play money.

"Just a minute, you dumb[2] Orange!" he cried. "What are you doing bothering[3] this Blue? Get back to your seat and don't dare enter blue territory again or you'll be sorry!"

Adam hesitated, then grinned, clicking[3] his heels together. *"Jawohl mein Kommandant!"*

"Bow before you leave, Orange! Bow to the female Blue!"

"You're kidding!"

"Record keeper ... get this Orange's name."

"Adam, please. Don't get into trouble. Remember what you said about moving up," I pleaded.

Adam bowed, his face a deep shade of pink. I hated being bowed to, especially by him, and looked away.

"Blue!" Mary called out. "In the future you report it when an inferior addresses you without permission! Understand? Now, lead the other Blues out, please."

I began to tremble, unused to such harsh criticism made so publicly.

"Come on, girl," Paul said, nudging me. "Let's go! Those lowly Oranges aren't worth a bag o' beans." He lapsed into black jive. "They's nothin' but lowdown lazy bums[3] who won't work for a living an' just waste the big taxes us rich folk pay!"

I gathered up my books, eyes on Adam, who had returned to his seat. With an uneasy pain in my stomach I led the Blues ... all six of us, all minorities ... out the door.

17 **to plead** to say very urgently and seriously; to beg – 25 **to nudge** to push gently, especially with one's elbow – 26 **o'** of – **to lapse into** to slip into; to start using – **jive** a kind of American slang spoken by Blacks – **they's** *(slang)* they are – 27 **lowdown** worthless

Chapter 4

Something had happened in that strange exchange that confused and upset me. But it wasn't until free period that I could get off by myself to think. Sitting at a back table in the library with my books open but unread, it began to make sense.

All I cared about lately was what Adam wanted, thought, or felt. When I didn't agree with him, I swallowed my words and said nothing, sometimes even smiling approval. It seemed my whole self-image depended on Adam's opinion of me.

What about what I thought, wanted, or felt?

But boys didn't like girls to have too many ideas of their own. I'd learned that two summers ago at a special Japanese camp Mama and Papa sent me to. They wanted me to mix with other Japanese kids and learn something about our culture. And I had learned, about calligraphy and origami and the tea ceremony and holidays, and even some Japanese. But what had made the greatest impression was what I'd learned about being "female."

The most popular girls, it became clear, weren't always the prettiest. They were the sweet, agreeable, non-threatening ones, those who made the boys feel strong, smart, and important. Girls who didn't play that role weren't likely to have boyfriends.

It didn't take long to see, even in high school, that most boys liked girls that way. So, I became a chameleon[2]. I adapted to whomever I dated. And after a while I hardly knew what *I* really felt and thought because I became so good at adapting.

Adam had bowed to me. He'd been forced to, and he'd hated it. Yet I bowed to him all the time in all kinds of ways. Why? Staring at my hands as I sat thinking in the library I remembered his most recent urging. "Just be bad and you'll get demoted, and I'll be good and get promoted."

That would bring us together at some in-between color.

I hadn't protested. By silence I'd agreed. Yet a small knife had twisted in my stomach then, and did again now, because that wasn't what I wanted. It wasn't in my nature to try to fail. As wonderful as it would be going through the game with Adam, I really wanted to be Dark

2 **period** *(AE)* lesson *(BE)* – 13 **calligraphy** [kə'lɪgrəfɪ] art of producing beautiful handwriting – 14 **origami** [ˌɒrɪ'gɑːmɪ] Japanese art of paper folding – 18 **non-threatening** not putting into danger – 28 **urging** the act of trying very hard to persuade s.o. – 31 **to twist** to turn

Green or Blue, not a lower color. And now I had that chance. Why shouldn't I savor the experience, play the Blue, and see how it felt having power and privileges[2] I'd never had, power and privileges Adam had every day of his life?

I'd tell him, but would it make him angry? And could I actually free that "me" trapped[3] so long inside the person pleaser[1], the father pleaser, and now the Adam pleaser?

I bit my lip and stared out the window at a liquidambar tree shedding its fall colors[3] against a clear blue sky. It was only a game, and for only four weeks, as Adam had pointed out. I would try to convince him we should play the game as it should be played and not try to fix it for our own benefit.

At lunchtime I stood on tiptoe[1], craning to search for Adam above the heads of students in the line. Usually, he arrived first. His last class was only three doors down from the cafeteria. He could often tell what was on the menu each day just from the smells which reached his math class.

But today, for whatever reason, Adam was late. I stepped out of line as one of the boys who sat at our lunch table went by with his tray. "Rob? You see Adam?"

"Yeah. He was in line right behind me when this girl comes up with a green band on her arm and says, "Back of the line, Orange!" Rob's eyes scanned[3] the lunch crowd. "I couldn't believe it. Adam bowed to her like she was royalty, or something. Then he goes to the back of the line. What's going on, Amy?"

"Tell you later." I moved slowly along the lunch line searching for Adam. A light green armband caught my eye. Odd, how I checked arms before looking at faces since getting my own blue band. "Justin?" I touched him. "Have you seen Adam?"

Justin's face flushed[3] as he glanced at my band. For an instant he seemed uncertain what to do. Then, with a flourish, he bowed before answering, "He's in back with the Oranges."

I was about to look further when I stopped myself. Why this ridiculous frantic feeling? Hadn't I just resolved to play the game exactly as

2 **to savor** ['seɪvə] (*BE* savour) to enjoy s.th. slowly – 8 **liquidambar** [ˌlɪkwɪd'æmbə] **tree** tree with a pleasant smell, the wood of which is often used for furniture – **to shed, shed, shed** to let fall or come off – 9 **fall** *(AE) autumn* – 12 **benefit** ['benɪfɪt] profit, advantage – 13 **to crane** to stretch one's neck to get a better view – 31 **with a flourish** ['flʌrɪʃ] with a showy movement to get attention – 34 **frantic** anxious, excited – **to resolve** to decide firmly

Otero had set it up, to try to be independent of Adam for a while? Even if I reached him, we couldn't talk. G4's might be watching. Others could report me and I didn't want to be demoted. Not now.

I turned about and went back to my place in line. If Adam and I couldn't talk at the lunch table, there was the telephone and other places where we might not be seen. Resolutely[2], I picked up a tray and piled[1] on a tossed salad, strawberry yogurt[2], and a container[1] of milk.

Justin arrived at the lunch table before Adam did. He set his tray down on my side of the table, with Penny, Rob's girlfriend, between us.

"What are those funny bands you guys are wearing?" Melissa asked, echoing the curiosity of the others. "Is that the Color Game you were talking about?" She addressed the question to Justin, although sitting opposite me.

Melissa never spoke directly to me if she could help it, I thought with a stir of annoyance. There was a pecking order of some kind. She'd address Adam first, if he was present, then Justin, then Rob, then any other girls, before me.

"I'm a lowly Light Green," Justin said. "You know, in the same class with the enchiladas." He laughed.

I hated it when Justin called Latinos that. Did he call me *rice cake* or *slant eyes* when I wasn't around?

"Light Greens don't speak up[3] when Blues are present," I said lightly, surprised at how angry I felt. It would do Justin good to get a taste of his own superior attitude, but under the table my legs began shivering[3].

"Hey, Amy ..." Justin protested.

"Well, how *does* it work?" Melissa asked again, addressing me this time. It felt good explaining the game with everyone listening. Just because I wore a blue armband!

Adam slipped his tray down next to mine, then immediately turned away. "Where are you going?" I called after him. He waved a hand in reply and wove through the noisy lunch room to Paul Thomas's table. Something Paul said brought loud laughter from the other black students and a low bow from Adam. Then Adam picked up Paul's tray and took it to the refuse can. He dumped[3] the paper plates and napkins in the bin, left the tray, then returned to our table, scowling.

7 **tossed salad** fresh salad mixed with salad dressing – 16 **stir** slight feeling – **annoyance** irritation – **pecking order** order of seniority or power; hierarchy – 22 **slant** at an angle, not straight – 36 **refuse** ['refju:s] **can** *(AE)* rubbish bin *(BE)* – 37 **to scowl** [skaʊl] to have an angry look on one's face

"Boy, I've had it!" he exclaimed. "All I've done since third period is bow and run errands for higher colors. And now I gotta put up with Thomas's smart-ass jokes."

"What did he say?"

Adam swung his long legs over the bench and sat beside me, face still flushed with anger. "How many Oranges does it take to screw[3] in a light bulb?" He laughed bitterly. "You know. One to hold the bulb and nine to turn the chair."

"Fun-ny!" Justin said, "coming from *them!*"

"But that's the whole point, Justin," Adam said. "We make jokes like that about them all the time. It sure doesn't feel very good being on the receiving end[3]."

"They deserve it, though. If they weren't so lazy they could have what we got. Nobody in America has to be poor."

"I'm not so sure," Adam said, biting into a sandwich. "My father's always saying that. It's easy to say when you've got a multimillion-dollar business handed down by your grandfather, and when you're white with roots in Plymouth Rock."

"Ah, it's time those guys stopped blaming their poverty on color. Who's stopping them from going to college or working hard? I'm a Light Green now, but just watch me get to be a Blue. All I gotta do is figure out the system, then do whatever I gotta. If I have to kiss ass, so …"

"That's what the blacks in the South did during slavery days," I said quietly. "Yas'm, yas'm …" I craned my head around Penny to meet Justin's eyes. "It sure didn't get *them* very far."

"Yas'm …" Justin replied, with mock servility. "Us black folks likes to serve yo' white folks. It's in our blood. Cain't hep it if white folks is smarter. …"

Melissa laughed appreciatively.

"Justin," I said, surprising myself. "I'm going to make life miserable for you, just to see how you'll like it. After all, 'Us Blues is lots smarter than yo' low-down Light Greens.'"

2 **to run errands** to make short trips to perform necessary tasks – 3 **smart-ass** *(AE slang)* know-it-all, arrogant – 18 **Plymouth** ['plɪməθ] **Rock** a large rock in Massachusetts said to be the landing place of the first English settlers (Pilgrims) in 1620 – 22 **to kiss ass** *(AE slang)* to be eager to obey and please those who are in a position of power – 25 **Yas'm** *(slave dialect)* yes, master – 27 **servility** exaggerated respect – 28 **cain't** *(African-American slang)* can't – **hep** *(African-American slang)* help – 30 **appreciatively** [ə'priːʃjətɪvlɪ] in a manner showing that one enjoys the qualities of s.th.

"Oh, *Justin!*" Rob cried. "Better watch out! Amy's got it in for you!"

"I'm scared. I'm really scared!" Justin pretended to shiver. "Can you imagine Adam's sweet, exotic Amy going after mean ole me?"

Adam laughed and kissed me on the side of the head. But that made me only angrier. So that's how Justin saw me, how the others thought of me. No wonder I often felt uncomfortable.

"Justin," I said sweetly. "I finished my lunch and I know you'd just love to put my tray away."

"I'm not done with my lunch."

"That's a shame, but Light Greens do what they're told to do *when* they're told, or they get reported to G4's, don't they?" My voice came out in a quaver, but I tried to keep a gentle smile on my lips. Everyone watched Justin as he seemed to struggle with himself over what to do. Then he shrugged, got up, and came behind me to pick up my tray.

"Before you leave, Justin," I added, trembling inside and determined not to show it, "you will of course bow to your superior." I gave him an especially sweet smile, trying to take the sting out of my words.

A dark look crossed his face. He grimaced[2] to show he was only humoring me, then swept his right arm in front of his stomach in a poor imitation of a bow.

The heat rose to my face at his attitude. "That was a pretty good bow, Justin, but I know you could do better. Why not try it again?"

Melissa held a hand over her mouth to hide her giggles, but the others were grinning openly. Justin bowed again, this time with an insolent flourish. I hesitated only a moment, then, bristling, said, "Again."

"I'll be damned if –!"

"What's going on here, Blue? Is this Light Green being impudent? What's your name, fella?" Brian, the G4, took out a small pad[3] and clicked a pen into readiness.

"It's nothing, Brian," I said quickly, afraid I'd gotten Justin in real trouble. "Everything's under control. We were just testing each other, that's all."

Had I gone too far? I sensed a chill at the table as Brian wrote Justin's name in a little book despite my protests, and it frightened me.

1 **to have (got) it in for s.o.** *(coll.)* to intend to harass or harm s.o. – 4 **mean** *(AE)* unkind, liking to hurt people – **ole** *(slang)* old – 13 **in a quaver** trembling – 15 **to shrug** to raise one's shoulders to show that one doesn't care – 18 **sting** s.th. that causes pain – 25 **insolent** disrespectful, impolite – 26 **to bristle** ['brɪsl] to show anger – 28 **impudent** ['ɪmpjʊdent] insolent – 34 **chill** an unpleasant feeling of coldness

Maybe I should apologize. I glanced uneasily at Adam as the bell rang, wishing he'd say something, anything, to make it all right. But he didn't. He hurriedly downed the last of his lunch and gathered up his things.

All my resolve to be more independent of him was forgotten. I wanted to know if he was angry with me, and when we'd get together again, and if he still loved me. But I said nothing and we hurried out of the lunch room together like total strangers. When we parted at fifth-period class Adam seemed distant and preoccupied.

"Will you call?" I asked, ashamed to be the aggressor[2] by asking.

Adam glanced around the crowded hall as if expecting to be reported, then touched my hand briefly. "I'll try." With that he rushed away.

I waited for his phone call all afternoon. Was this the day he had soccer practice? And afterward swimming? Was that why he didn't call? Or was it the day he met with the student-body council after school? I chopped the vegetables for dinner, set the table with flowers from Mama's garden, did my homework, and planned what I would cover when I tutored Bettina this week. Maybe Adam could arrange to be there so we could touch for a moment, if Bettina left us alone. But no matter what work I did, Adam's silence felt like punishment.

I jumped when the phone rang and grabbed[3] it before it could ring a second time.

"Adam?" I held my breath, waiting for his answer. I'd know instantly if he was angry.

"Hi, Amy. You speaking with a lowly Orange, or should I bow first?"

It was all right. Still, I had to ask. "Are you angry with me?"

"For what you said to Justin? He's had that coming for a long time. It was just a surprise, that's all. Nobody's used to you speaking up like that."

I took a deep breath. The kitchen seemed brighter, warmer, than before. "I don't think I like being a Blue. You have to be so heartless.

1 **to apologize** to say one is sorry for having done s.th. bad – 5 **resolve** firm decision, determination – 9 **preoccupied** so worried about s.th. that one pays no attention to anything else – 14 **soccer** European football – 16 **student-body council** *Schülermitverwaltung* – 17 **to chop** [tʃɒp] to cut into small pieces – 18 **to cover** *here:* to deal with – 28 **he's had that coming** *(coll.)* he deserves this and I'm glad it happened to him

I mean, this business of being mean[3] to lower colors just so they'll get a taste of what it's really like for others … it's just not natural for me. I don't like people bowing to me. It's not comfortable."

"You can get demoted, you know." When I didn't answer, he added, "Didn't you once tell me your grandfather said everyone in Japan bows to everyone else?"

I nodded, though Adam couldn't see. "But that's different. When *everyone* bows, it shows respect, but if only *some* do, those who *have to* feel inferior. Like you must have when Paul …"

"Yeah, that was rough. I never thought much about poor people, minorities. I always figured most people felt good about who they were, like I did. Then today … I felt ashamed. As if I was dirt. …"

"Yeah," I said. "I know." There had been times when I'd been made to feel ugly and unworthy just because I wasn't white and the pain had been terrible. But I had learned how to deal[3] with it. Now, whenever I met someone new I showed only a small, protected part of myself until I could be sure. Even then, it took time for me to trust.

It was hard to admit, but sometimes I wished I were white.

"Adam?" My voice sounded funny as I gathered[3] courage to say what I had decided. "I'm going to try to stay a Blue."

Adam's silence frightened me. "Do you mind terribly? I just want to find out what it's like," I went on hurriedly. "And really, it won't change me. I mean, I'm not going on a power trip[3] or anything. …"

"Amy, do your realize what that means? We won't be able to be together for weeks!"

"I know, I know … and worse, you'll have to bow to me and pretend to be subservient … and I'll hate that … but you'll know I don't mean anything by it, that it's just a role I have to play for a while."

"Why? You just said you didn't like having people bow to you!"

"I don't! But … but … it's hard to explain!" I pushed my hair back with nervous fingers. "Everyone says that the rich don't care about anyone else; all they care about is getting richer. Well, maybe that's not true. I want to see if I can't … do something."

"Oh." Adam paused, as if thinking, then said, "Like what?"

"I don't really know … talk to the other Blues, see what we could do to break down those color barriers. It doesn't have to be the way Otero says it is!"

"In the meantime, what about us?"

10 **rough** [rʌf] very unpleasant – 27 **subservient** [səbˈsɜːvjənt] always willing to obey or do what others want

"I can see you when I tutor Bettina ... and maybe we could see each other Sunday ... somewhere not so public so we're not likely to run into any class members or G4's ..."

"I don't like it. I thought you could do something outrageous so they'd throw you out of the Blues." He paused. "Why should we put up with it? I don't mind playing the game while I'm at school, but why should we go along with it outside?"

"I guess because prejudice goes on twenty-four hours a day."

Adam answered with an unconvinced "Ummm."

"Otero says that of all the students who've played the game so far, only five quit[3], and of those, three dropped[3] because of program conflicts."

"Maybe they stay because of peer pressure."

"It's more than that, Adam. Otero's a good guy. I think we all know that. I think he's trying to get something across[3] to us that we couldn't get any other way. I kind of feel – we can't let him down."

Adam breathed a loud protesting sigh, but said, "If that's what you want, okay, but I'll hate it, having this fence between us for the next few weeks."

I let out a small yelp[3] of pleasure. "Oh, Adam, thanks! I'd hug you if you were here right now, hug you so tight you'd melt!"

"So what's stopping you?"

I smiled happily at the phone. "Close your eyes. Now listen. I'm putting my arms around your neck ... and getting as close as I can ... and ..."

"Amy Sumoto," Adam purred. "You're crazy ... and I'm crazy about you. Now, tell me. When are you coming to tutor Bettina?"

4 **outrageous** [aʊt'reɪdʒəs] very shocking – 9 **unconvinced** doubtful, showing disbelief – 13 **peer** person of the same age or position – 17 **sigh** [saɪ] letting out breath to express disappointment – 26 **to purr** *here:* to speak in a low voice to show pleasure (*usu. of cats:* to produce a low sound to express peasure)

Chapter 5

Adam and I couldn't walk together openly anymore because we might be reported. That proved to be the hardest adjustment to make from the start of the Color Game. Being reported wouldn't have hurt *me* so much, because Blues, Otero said, are treated differently by society, with respect and tolerance. Adam, though, would be the one who'd be punished. He'd be fined and made a fool of and who knows what else.

It made me wonder if Adam and I could have ever become friends in real life if one of us had been very poor. We'd have so little in common because where we live makes us what we are. Friends are made, usually, among those you have most in common with. How can a really rich person find much in common with someone very poor? I think that money, or the lack of it, makes more of a difference between people than color.

When we got to Otero's class the next day, all my antennae stood up, trying to sense who might report us. The rest of the class were waiting for Otero, but in different groupings from the day before. This time the Blues – all black and Latino – were closest to the front door, and Adam's group, the Oranges, stood apart.

"Well, Amy ..." Brian stepped into place beside me, ignoring Adam. A senior, and sports editor of the school paper, he had danced with me at the luau until Adam told him the rest of the dances were taken. Brian said, "I see you're wearing your armband, Amy. Very good. How about your journal?"

I fished inside my notebook and brought out the new pink pad.

"Glad you're following the rules. You going to the Halloween dance, by the way?"

Adam and I had planned to go to the Halloween dance together weeks ago, before Otero's class. I bit my lip. Could we still attend if we weren't supposed to socialize because of our colors? "Well, I don't know," I said, noting Adam's frown.

"Want to go with *me?*"

"Bug off!" Adam exclaimed. "She's my girl, Brian!"

15 **antennae** [æn'teni:] *pl.* organs of touch on the head of an insect *(Fühler)* – 21 **editor** person who checks and corrects texts before they are published – 26 **Halloween** [ˌhæləʊ'i:n] evening of October 31 when children in costume go from door to door asking for sweets (often associated with ghosts and witches) – 31 **frown** displeased look – 33 **Bug off!** *(AE slang)* Go away!

"Who's talking to you, Orange? What are you doing even walking *near* a Blue?" Brian took out his small notebook and marked something down as Otero trotted along the hall fumbling among his keys.

"What about it, Amy?"

"Thanks, but I think I'll pass."

"Take my advice. If you socialize with Oranges, your Blue friends are going to think less of you, even shun you. People who have anything to do with Oranges are either troublemakers or they have no respect for their own class."

"Oh, come on. You don't mean that!"

"Don't I?" Brian smiled at me again. "See you around."

"Creep ..." Adam grumbled as Brian strode ahead to the classroom door and called out:

"Blues first!"

I gave Adam an apologetic shrug and moved forward, slipping by classmates, whose eyes I avoided so they wouldn't have to bow. When I took my seat, Paul Thomas leaned over and in a loud voice asked, "How's about after class you and me stand right outside the door and make the whole class bow?"

"Paul, you're depraved," I said.

"Yeah, and loving it. I got this picture of myself now, y'know? *Thomas Industries.* That's me. Right there on the stock exchange. Got this house in Bel-Air, five acres and guard dogs all over, and this gorgeous wife who greets me at night in a slinky gown with a glass of Chivas Regal. The kids are in private school, and I drive a Rolls. And all these other guys, these other *colors,"* he said with distaste, "they're working for *me!* Those Dark Greens are practically panting to get my approval. The Light Greens tiptoe around like they're scared they'll be out on the street. And the Oranges. Well. That's what the guard dogs are for."

"Thomas, you *are* crazy. Mean, too!" I had to laugh. Paul seemed to have changed overnight. No more the guy slouching in his seat, trying to look as inconspicuous as possible. Having blue power seemed

5 **I'll pass** *here:* I'll not go this time – 7 **to shun s.o.** to keep away from, to avoid – 12 **creep** *(slang)* unpleasant person – **stride, strode, stridden** to walk with long steps – 15 **apologetic** [əˌpɒləˈdʒetɪk] showing that one is sorry for having done or said s.th. – 20 **depraved** morally bad, corrupt – 22 **stock exchange** *Börse* – 24 **gorgeous** very beautiful – **slinky** close to the body – 25 **Chivas Regal** an expensive brand of whisky – **Rolls** Rolls-Royce – 27 **to pant** *here:* to be extremely eager to do s.th. – 29 **to be out on the street** *here:* to lose one's job – 33 **inconspicuous** not easily noticed

to have brought out all kinds of sides to him – anger and spite against the poor and hope and ambition for himself.

Otero stepped in front of his desk and crossed his arms over his chest. "All right, guys. Now we come to sex discrimination. Teks and No-Teks. Mary, come up and explain, please."

Mary ambled to the front of the room and picked up a piece of chalk. "In Ray's game," she said, "the genders are reversed. The superior sex, called Teks, are the women." She wrote *Teks = women* on the board. "The inferior sex, men, are called No-Teks."

I laughed and the boys nearby groaned.

"No-Teks must curtsy to Teks of their color and higher colors. And if you don't know what a curtsy is, Brian will show you." With an insipid smile on his face Brian stepped forward, pretended to hold out a skirt, and bent one knee. "That's how No-Teks curtsy. Okay?" When no one objected, Mary went on. "No-Teks walk behind Teks and sit behind them in class. There is no one lower in this world than an Orange No-Tek. Not only is he in the lowest social class, but he's an insignificant gender, a male." Mary pushed her glasses against her face with one finger.

"Sometime during the next weeks we'll expect the No-Teks to bring coffee or tea to class, and to make and bring cookies."

"I can't even boil water!" Justin called out.

"You better learn fast!" Carol answered.

"... and the paper each Tek must write about her superiority, will be typed by a No-Tek."

"Hey, I like that!" one of the girls cried. "My boyfriend goes, 'Type this. Type that.' I go, 'How come you can't do it? You got fewer fingers than me?'"

It made me think. I had typed several papers for Adam and never thought anything of it, though it took time away from other things I could have done. Adam had taken typing. How come he didn't do it?

"... finally," Mary continued. "We'll have a No-Tek beauty contest. The men will be judged for their physical ... er ... attributes."

1 **spite** the desire to hurt s.o. in a small way – 7 **gender** the sex one belongs to – 11 **to curtsy** sign of respect made by women by bending the knees with one foot forward – 12 **insipid** without enthusiasm, flat – 15 **to object** to speak out against s.th. – 21 **cookies** *(AE)* biscuits *(BE)* – 24 **paper** *(AE) here:* essay, research paper – 26 **goes** *(slang)* says – 31 **typing** a course given in many American high schools where you can learn how to type – **how come** *(AE)* why

Her last words were drowned out by catcalls, squeals, and applause.

"... to repeat: for their physical attributes and ... er ... talents ... by a panel of Teks. I think that's all."

"Seating," Otero prompted.

"Oh, yes. No-Teks sit behind Teks, so all you males who are sitting beside or in front of a female of your color better change seats." The grumbling male class members picked up their books and moved about.

"And ... if you counted your money yesterday and compared it with what others got," Otero said above the uproar, "you'll note that Teks in each color got more than No-Teks of the same color, just as in society men often earn more than women who do the same work." He paused. "Now that we've set up our imaginary society as it really is, with the class you're born into largely deciding your future potential, and with the sex you're born into affecting your income and degree of subservience ... we can now begin to play the game. G4's, we'll have your reports now." The G4's came to the front of the room and one by one read from their books.

"Light Green Sharon Osborne was not wearing her color band in gym. Fined five dollars."

"Blue Paul Thomas has not purchased a journal yet, but we'll be lenient this time and expect him to bring his notebook tomorrow."

"Sure thing."

"Light Green Justin Charles does not have his journal yet. How come, Charles? The law is the law. You were told yesterday, like everyone else, to have that notebook, right?"

"Yes." Justin looked puzzled.

"Then where is it? Is your memory so bad you can't remember something so simple?"

"But I told you –"

"No excuses! Fined five dollars, and if you don't have it by tomorrow ..."

"You just excused Paul Thomas for the same thing!"

1 **to drown out** to prevent from being heard – **catcall** loud whistle or cry to express one's displeasure – **squeal** long high cry – 5 **to prompt** to remind s.o. what to say – 11 **uproar** ['ʌprɔ:] noise of angry people shouting – 16 **degree** *here:* level – 17 **subservience** behaving in such a way that one always obeys the wishes of people in a more important position – 22 **lenient** ['li:nɪənt] not severe or strict

"That's enough back talk, Light Green. Another word and I'll double that fine. Adam Tarcher?" The G4 ruffled through several pages. "You're an Orange? Yes. Tarcher, you were seen talking with a Blue on several occasions." He held up several slips of paper. "These were in the Fink Box. Stand up when you're spoken to!"

My heart beat anxiously as I turned around to see Adam, face flushed with embarrassment.

"What have you got to say, Orange?"

"Sue me."

I laughed with relief at Adam's good humor and control.

"My, my, we have a rebel in our midst," Bill said, smiling and scratching his head thoughtfully. "If the police had stopped you in real life, *Orange,* and you'd answered like that, you'd probably get shoved around a bit, then handcuffed and carted off to the pokey. But this is a game. So all we'll do is fine you fifteen bucks."

"Fifteen dollars!" Adam exclaimed. "Why, that's a fourth of the money I've got!"

"Isn't that a shame." Bill stared Adam down. "Next time maybe you won't talk back to your superiors. And if we have any more trouble from you, you *Orange No-Tek* ..." He drew the words out as if they were dirty. "You'll find we can make life pretty miserable. Sit down." He turned to me and in a gentle voice said, "Miss Sumoto ..."

I jumped up, ready to be punished as Bill reached my side. "We've had reports that you've been consorting with an Orange, Amy. We've also heard you don't demand the respect due you from your inferiors. You wouldn't want us to demote you, would you?" I stared at him, not answering. "Stick out your hand," he ordered. I put out my hand. He slapped the back of it lightly. "Now, let that be a lesson. And don't do it again."

Bill turned to a Dark Green, leaving me in a daze. Was that all? Adam fined and tongue-lashed and I get a mere tap on the wrist.

For the remaining period Otero lectured on racial injustice as it was handled in literature. He assigned reading material, a book on the

2 **to ruffle through** to quickly turn the pages – 5 **fink** *(AE)* person who informs on others – 9 **to sue** to start a legal case against s.o. – 11 **my, my** oh dear – 14 **to handcuff** to lock two connecting metal rings around a person's wrists – **pokey** ['pəʊkɪ] *(slang)* jail – 22 **gentle** soft, mild – 25 **due** what should be given to s.o. by right – 30 **in a daze** in a confused state – 31 **to tongue-lash** to criticize s.o. harshly – 33 **to assign** [ə'saɪn] to give as homework

black experience, one on the American Indians, one on the Latinos, and even one on the Japanese-American experience during World War II. The period ended in a whirl of confusion as students lined up according to color and sex. A black girl named Gwen and I were the only two Blue Teks, so we led the way from the room.

I walked down the hall slowly, hoping Adam would catch up and hoping he'd stay away so I'd not get him into more trouble. There had to be a way to sabotage Otero's game, to get everyone together to help each other regardless of the G4's. But how?

"Carol, wait!" I called, hurrying after my friend.

Carol stiffened as she slowed to my pace. Her eyes darted about anxiously.

"I want to talk to you."

"I'm not supposed to talk to Blues."

"You're not. *I'm* talking to *you*. That's allowed. All you have to do is say yes or no and you can't be reported."

Carol nodded, and we continued down the hall together. "Listen," I said. "I've been thinking. Let's all be friends. Blues, Dark Greens, Light Greens, and Oranges. There's no reason we should turn against each other just to prove Otero's right about society. What if I united the Blues and you did the same with the Dark Greens and we'd try to help the other colors?"

"How? Dark Greens aren't supposed to talk to Blues."

"So we'll meet secretly."

An Orange passing by caught our eyes and bowed, then hurried away. "I don't know," Carol said.

"Why? Surely you can't believe in all this!"

"I don't want to get into trouble and be demoted. In fact today Mary said I was prime material for becoming a Blue." She stood taller and smiled.

"But don't you hate how they're treating the lower colors?" I persisted.

Carol shrugged. "It won't hurt those rich white kids to know what it's like for us. *They* only have to live like that for four weeks." She lowered her voice as Brian came into view.

"Then you won't help?"

6 **to catch up** to reach s.o. who is ahead – 9 **regardless** without paying attention to – 11 – **pace** speed – **to dart about** to move about quickly – 29 **prime** excellent – 31 **to persist** [pə'sɪst] to continue to do s.th. in spite of opposition or failure

"No."

"Will you at least think about it?"

Brian stopped a little way down the hall and leaned against the wall, watching us.

"Carol?"

"Sorry, Amy, but no. I want to play the game the way it's supposed to be played. Gotta go." She gave me an apologetic smile, then hurried away.

I stood there in the middle of the nearly empty hall watching Carol's retreating back. Brian stopped her and then wrote something in a small notebook, looking my way.

Would Carol have reported our conversation? I got cold shivers down my back. Was it possible? Did she want that much to be a Blue that she'd fink on a friend?

10 **retreating** moving away

Chapter 6

"Let's talk about boys now," Bettina said, tilting her blond head charmingly at me. "There's this boy in my class. He goes, 'You got a cute nose.'"

"Tina! You find more ways to waste time! Why don't you finish this problem and then we'll talk."

Tutoring Adam's sister could easily be a time of fun and games, because Bettina thought up more ways to avoid working than I could ever imagine. In the last half hour she had taken a bathroom break, gone to sharpen a pencil, then to find out when her mother was coming home. And now she wanted to talk about boys. But I was determined to make Tina understand fractions even if it took twice the time I'd be paid for.

As Bettina picked up her pencil, sighing deeply, I felt a pang of affection. She looked so much like Adam with those clear blue eyes and golden hair. She even had many of his mannerisms, like peering up at me with lowered head. But they were very different. Bettina had little else on her mind except boys, and that childlike sweetness could change in a minute to vicious meanness if she didn't get her way.

"Three eighths plus five sixths equals ... umh ..." Bettina nibbled the end of her pencil and watched me secretly for signs of softening. "His name is David, and when he said that, I go –"

"Tina, do the problem. Come on. I'm not paid to talk about boys," I said.

Bettina bent thoughtfully over the paper, writing in a number, then checking my face, erasing the number, chewing her pencil, then writing again. At last she turned the page around for me to see.

"That's good!" I said. "I told you you could do it! All you have to do is concentrate."

"I'll flunk the test tomorrow. I just know it. I'm terrible in math."

"Never mind, you'll pass the test tomorrow, and you could be good at math. Whoever said you couldn't?"

1 **to tilt** to move down to one side – 3 **cute** [kju:t] *(AE)* sweet, attractive – 8 **bathroom** *(AE)* toilet – 11 **fraction** numbers such as $^1/_2$, $^5/_8$ etc. – 13 **pang** sudden sharp feeling, usually of pain – **affection** fondness, liking – 15 **to peer** to look, to gaze – 18 **vicious** ['vɪʃəs] hateful – **meanness** *(AE)* the quality of wanting to hurt others – 19 **nibble** to each with small bites – 29 **to flunk** *(AE)* to fail a test or examination

"Girls aren't good at things like that. My mother says so. It's unfeminine."

"*I'm* good at math. Am I unfeminine?"

Bettina raised one shoulder in a shrug and watched me with an odd intensity. "You're different."

"How?"

"You're ... *Oriental.*" Bettina wet her lips and smiled slyly. "Mother says Orientals have special aptitudes for math and science."

So that's what they said about me when I wasn't around. Should I be pleased, even proud? A warning bell went off in my head and the warmth I'd felt moments ago changed to caution. Friends, real friends, didn't make remarks like that. What else did Mrs. Tarcher say about *Orientals,* I wondered? How many of her prejudices had Adam absorbed?

"Well isn't that true about ... Orientals?"

"People are people, whatever their race or color. There's no special aptitude one class of people has over another, *Oriental* or not. And there's no reason why women can't be as good at math or science as men."

Bettina shook her blond curls impatiently. "I'm sick of talking about that. I finished the problem, so now let's talk about this boy I know."

I put the math book away and threw the scratch papers in a basket as Bettina scurried from the desk to jump on her white-canopied bed. She reached for a large stuffed bear and hugged it to her chest, eyes rolled to heaven.

"David ... mmm ... this boy at school ..." Her eyes shone. "I think he likes me, but I'm not sure. ..." Bettina went on to relate each word the boy had ever spoken to her, what she thought about him, what she thought he thought about her, what her girlfriends said, and on and on.

I gazed around the spacious room, soothed as always by its rich carpeting and furnishings. But my thoughts were on the time. Normally I left the house right after the hour of tutoring, before Adam got home. But today I'd promised to stay as long as possible in case Adam

7 **slyly** in a tricky or dishonest way – 8 **aptitude** ability, talent – 11 **caution** quality of being careful in order to avoid danger – 23 **scratch paper** *(AE)* paper already used on one side that is used again for taking notes, etc. – 24 **canopied** ['kænəpɪd] with a covering over a bed held up by posts – 32 **to soothe** [su:ð] to make calm and more comfortable – 33 **furnishings** furniture, curtains, etc.

could leave soccer practice early. We hadn't been alone together since Otero's class began, more than a week before. I felt almost a desperate need to feel his arms around me again.

"So, what do you think?" Bettina asked finally, bringing my attention back. "Should I go around with him? Not steady or anything – you know, just going around ..."

"Did you hear a car?" I asked, going to the window.

"Amy! You're not even listening! You're just hoping my brother will get home!" Bettina threw the bear at me. "Now, pay attention! Does he like me or not?"

I lifted the big toy off the floor and put it back on the bed, then picked up my purse and book. "I think it's time for me to go, Tina. Please tell Adam I'm sorry I couldn't wait." I started to the door. "And as for David, you might try backing off a bit. Boys don't like girls who come on too strong." I paused at the door. "Good luck on the test tomorrow, Tina. See you next week."

I hurried down the long hall on the highly waxed floors smelling of lemon, wishing I could stop to examine each beautiful painting on the walls between the many doors. But I didn't dare. What if Mrs. Tarcher came out of one of the rooms and saw me? Far away somewhere I heard a grandfather clock chime and distant voices amid the sounds of pots clashing. How could I feel so comfortable with Adam when I felt so uncomfortable in this, his home? And where was he? Why hadn't he got home early, as planned?

I stood at the top of the wide stairway leading to the entry and for a moment imagined myself the mistress of this house. With my hair piled high I'd be dressed in a filmy gown and Adam would be waiting at the bottom step. Slowly, head high, with one hand on the polished oak banister, I drifted down the stairs.

"Amy!"

"Oh! Mrs. Tarcher!" The blood raced to my face. I felt as if she'd caught me with the family silver.

Dressed in a beige linen suit, she stood at the foot of the stairs looking past me as if expecting Adam to be there.

"How's Tina doing?" she asked, reaching for a packet of mail on the entry table.

5 **to go steady with s.o.** to go out with a girl/boy regularly – 21 **grandfather clock** tall clock in wooden casing that stands on the floor – 22 **to clash** to make a loud noise as when two metal objects hit each other – 27 **filmy** so thin that one can see through it – **gown** [gaʊn] long dress worn for formal occasions – 29 **oak** *Eiche* – **banister** rail to hold on to along the side of a staircase

"Fine. I think she understands fractions now." I hurried down the last steps and crossed the entry hall.

"Good ... good." The voice was distracted. Then Mrs. Tarcher glanced at her watch. "It's rather late, isn't it?"

"Yes, I stayed a little longer. Tina has a test tomorrow and I wanted to be sure ..." I put a hand on the doorknob, wanting to flee.

"Yes ... well, thank you ... er, Eileen. We really appreciate all you've done." Mrs. Tarcher's gray eyes met mine for an instant and crinkled into a polite smile. "We'll see how Tina does in that test, then call you if we feel she needs more coaching." Her attention returned to the letters in hand.

She didn't even remember my name. She'd mixed me up with that Eileen Conley she wanted Adam to date! I was being dismissed and might not be returning.

Shouldn't I be paid? Each time I came no one said anything and it was embarrassing to ask. Papa had said, "Embarrassed? Why? It's your due. Rich people sometimes forget others depend on money to live. You earned it. Ask!"

Mrs. Tarcher looked up, surprised to see me still waiting. "Is there something else?"

"Uhm, yes, Mrs. Tarcher. I've tutored Tina six times now and you said I'd be ... paid ..."

"Of course you'll be paid!" Adam's mother exclaimed. "I'll write you a check right now if you like."

"Oh, no. That's not necessary," I quickly amended. "You can mail it to me whenever it's convenient."

The cool gray eyes settled briefly on me. "Well good-bye, then, er ... dear. And thanks again for your help." She had already turned away as I opened the door.

Hurrying down the driveway to the gate in the growing darkness, I felt such a mix of emotions. Shame over my encounter with Mrs. Tarcher. Disappointment that Adam hadn't gotten away from soccer practice in time. Frustration that we got to see so little of each other.

3 **distracted** not paying attention; as if thinking of s.th. else – 6 **knob** [nɒb] round handle on a door to open and shut it – 7 **to appreciate** to recognize the good qualities of s.th. – 8 **to crinkle** to become covered with fine lines or folds – 13 **to dismiss** to send away or allow to go – 17 **due** s.th. that should be given to s.o. by right – 25 **to amend** [əˈmend] to correct what had been said or written before – 26 **convenient** [kənˈviːnjənt] suitable, not causing any difficulties – 30 **driveway** private road that connects a house with the street – 31 **encounter** unexpected meeting – 32 **gotten** *(AE)* (past participle) got *(BE)*

No matter where we went it seemed like a hundred eyes were always watching, ready to report us.

A police car cruised by, slowing to look me over as I unlatched the gate. And then I heard the happy beep-beep of Adam's BMW!

Adam screeched to the curb, opened the door, and jumped out. I rushed into his arms with a yelp of joy and buried my face in his chest.

"Amy, Amy ..." he whispered again and again into my hair. "I thought I'd never get away. Coach wanted to go over every single play. I kept watching the clock and cutting everyone short, knowing you were waiting."

"I thought you'd forgotten. I waited as long as I could. I thought we'd miss each other again. And then your mother ..."

"It's all right; it's all right." He smoothed my hair with his hand. "We're together now." He drew me back to the car, kissed me and kissed me as if he couldn't get enough, then opened the door and helped me in. He ran around to the driver's side, climbed in, and reached for me again. We clung together, laughing and kissing, starting sentences and stopping them with each happy embrace.

"Now, what's this about my mother?" he asked at last when I curled against his shoulder.

It was so good between us now I didn't want to spoil things. "Nothing, oh, nothing really."

"No, tell me! Did she say something that hurt you? Come on, tell me."

My voice broke as I said, "It's how she makes me feel. She acts almost as if I'm invisible. She called me 'Eileen.' It's so obvious she thinks I'm not good enough for you!"

"Oh, honey, don't cry, please. My mother's the world's least sensitive woman. I've told you that. Who cares what she thinks?"

"I do! I care what my parents think, too, and they're just as unhappy about me seeing you!"

Adam pointed to himself. "Me? They don't like *me* – such a clean, upstanding WASP like me?"

"It's not funny. Please don't joke about it!"

3 **to cruise** [kru:z] to move along slowly - **to unlatch** *aufklinken* – 5 **to screech** to make a loud noise when stepping on the brakes – 8 **play** *Spielzug* – 9 **to cut s.o. short** to interrupt s.o.; not to let s.o. finish what he/she wanted to say – 13 **to smooth** [smu:ð] to make s.th. even or flat – 20 **to curl** *here:* to lean against – 28 **sensitive** respecting the feelings of other people – 33 **upstanding** honest, respectable, responsible – **WASP** White Anglo-Saxon Protestant, i.e. s.o. in the class considered to have controlling influence in American society

Adam's face sobered. "Talking about trouble, I feel like that's all I'm into since this Color Game started. Yesterday Carol insisted I curtsy to her, right in front of my French teacher. When I made a joke of it, she got angry and I had to do it, making me feel like two cents!" Adam pulled me closer, as if seeking comfort. "I was rewarded yesterday. You know why? For being *submissive* when a G4 chewed me out. I feel sick just thinking about it!"

"Is it really so awful?"

"Bowing is nothing. I do that automatically now, like brushing my teeth. What really gets to me is the constant feeling of being out of step with authority, the G4's, the upper colors. I've lived a Blue all my life, yet now I feel really threatened! I go around smiling a lot, as if everything's great, but inside I'm on guard, watching all the time, sure I'll do something that I'll get called down for." He stared at me for a long moment. "Do you suppose most poor people and minorities feel that way a lot of the time?"

"I don't know. We're not poor. I *do* know we all wear masks. We smile when we're miserable, pretend to like people we don't; and being nonwhite puts you even more on guard. Being poor ... it's hard to keep your self-respect because it's the American way to 'have' ..." I tried to remember the few times I'd learned about people outside of my own narrow world of aunts, uncles, and close family.

"Once, when I was about Bettina's age, I went with my father to visit a man he knew who had lost an arm in an auto accident. He was a lathe operator, I think, so losing his arm was a terrible thing because he couldn't work at that again. I remember a strange feeling in that house. Almost an odor ... fear. It was in the way the children crept around watching and whispering; it was in his wife's eyes and stiffness. It was as if the whole family stood on the edge of a terrible crater and might fall in at any moment."

"What happened to them?"

"Papa said they'd 'survive', that the mother would have to go to work and in time the husband would find some way to help. But that all their dreams for a better life were smashed with that arm because now all they could do was struggle to keep food on the table."

1 **to sober** to become serious and thoughtful – 6 **submissive** willing to obey – **to chew s.o. out** *(AE)* to criticize s.o. severely – 13 **on guard** [gɑːd] watching out for danger – 14 **to get called down for s.th.** to get into trouble for s.th. – 25 **lathe** [leɪð] **operator** *Dreher* – 27 **odor** ['əʊdə] (*BE* odour) smell, usually unpleasant – **to creep, crept, crept** to move slowly and quietly – 27 **stiffness** tension – 34 **to smash** to break into pieces – 35 **to struggle** to fight

Adam said nothing, staring thoughtfully out of the window, and in the dim light I wondered what he was thinking.

"I remember most of what Papa said later," I added. "In America, and maybe everywhere in the world, we're judged by two things ... by how much money we have ... and by our color. Money is power. If you have enough of it people won't forget your color but they'll at least *pretend* to."

Adam nodded. "Yes. Maybe that's why I feel so inadequate. Otero's set it up so Oranges have so little money to begin with that we're scared we'll lose the little we have. I'm not used to feeling ... insecure. I thought, when the game started, that all I had to do was work hard and I'd move up. People do. My grandfather started as a poor English immigrant, and look what he built! But I'm not willing to take garbage, to grovel. From now on I'm going to fight the system, somehow!"

"How?" I turned toward him so I could see his face better. Suddenly I had a terrible thought – that I should report Adam's plans to the G4's. Blues wanted to keep things as they were, and if there was unrest ... any sign of uprisings or protest among the poor ... they needed to know about it. As soon as the thought surfaced, I pushed it away. How could I even *think* of betraying Adam?

A light flashed through our window and then a police car pulled up alongside. I sat straighter and inched away from Adam into the shadows.

A policeman beamed his light into our car, illuminating Adam's face, then mine.

"Is there some problem, officer?" Adam asked without a trace of fear or servility.

"This is a no-parking area. May I see your license, please?"

Adam didn't even reach for his wallet. "I live here. I'm Adam Tarcher."

"Oh, Mr. Tarcher, I wasn't sure!" The policeman's manner changed abruptly and he started to put his notebook away. He glanced at me

2 **dim** not bright – 8 **inadequate** [ɪn'ædɪkwət] unable to deal with s.th. – 9 **to set s.th. up** to arrange – 10 **insecure** not feeling safe or certain – 13 **to take garbage** ['gɑ:bɪdʒ] *(AE)* to be treated badly, to be humiliated – 14 **to grovel** to show extreme respect to people in power – 20 **to surface** ['sɜ:fɪs] *here:* to come into one's mind – 21 **to betray** to be disloyal, to give information to the enemy – 23 **to inch away** to move away slowly – 28 **servility** being too ready to obey others in power – 30 **wallet** small flat leather case for carrying paper money

but spoke to Adam. "Just checking, you know. Don't like strangers loitering in this neighborhood."

I tugged at Adam's sleeve and whispered, "I have to get home, Adam. It's late." A memory of another time and place started me shivering. Hideo had been stopped by a policeman on a motorcycle. The officer's manner hadn't been so polite. Before he left us he chewed Hideo out and gave him a ticket. This policeman wouldn't do that. Not to Adam, one of the Valley Vista kids.

"We'll be leaving in a moment, officer. Thanks for checking," Adam said.

"No trouble." The policeman got back into his car and in a moment drove away. Suddenly I hated being in this neighborhood, getting privileged treatment just because of Adam. It made me feel alien and vulnerable and angry. I could hardly wait to get home.

2 **to loiter** to stand or wait around for no purpose – 7 **ticket** *here: Strafzettel* – 13 **alien** ['eɪljən] as if one doesn't belong – 14 **vulnerable** ['vʌlnərəbl] easily hurt or attacked

Chapter 7

That evening I phoned Carol. My head buzzed with all kinds of half-formed thoughts to talk with her about. I couldn't really accept that she'd be willing to forget old friends just because she was a Dark Green trying to move up. I wished she'd want to help the lower colors. After all, she knew what it was to be poor and a minority, to be always put down.

"Want to go shopping with me tomorrow?" I asked. One of the things we used to do before Adam and I became so close was browse around the shopping mall on a Saturday and stop for lunch at the taco stand, where Carol said the tacos were almost as good as those her mother made at home.

"I don't know," she said quickly. "Where?"

"The mall, I thought. There's a new store opened for teens. Melissa says they have some cute things."

"We might be seen. I don't want to be reported."

"Oh, Carol!" I protested. "We're upper class. The G4's hardly pay any attention to us anymore. Besides, what would you lose? You'll get criticized, or maybe fined a few dollars."

"That's easy for you to say. You're a Blue and they won't penalize *you.*"

I sighed. It was very clear from her attitude that there wasn't the slightest chance she'd be open to an idea I'd been playing with. Yet I couldn't give up. Carol was one of the most thoughtful, caring people I'd ever met. You don't just change personality because of a *game.* "Maybe we could meet somewhere else. If I could borrow Hideo's car for a couple of hours, we could drive to the Beverly mall. That's far enough away to be safe."

"Maybe."

"What do you mean, *maybe?* Maybe you'll come, or maybe it's safe?"

"Well, you know, Amy. We can't always tell if someone's a G4, can we?"

1 **to buzz** to make a continuous sound like a bee – 8 **to browse** [braʊz] **around** to walk around looking at things without any clear purpose – 9 **shopping mall** *(AE)* large shopping center usually under a roof – **taco** [ˈtɑːkəʊ] Mexican dish made with thin crispy corn bread and meat – 19 **to penalize** [ˈpiːnəlaɪz] to punish

I didn't answer. My silence must have reached her conscience because she finally said, "Oh, shoot! It *is* stupid not being able to talk. It's funny. I'm able to talk to a whole lot of people who never noticed me before, just because I'm Dark Green and they're lower colors than me. I'm even finding they're kind of nice." She thought a moment, then giggled. "You know what? It's kind of ridiculous. I'll meet you, why not?"

"Wonderful!"

"Sure. And let's be daring. Let's leave our armbands and notebooks home and the devil with the Color Game. In fact, let's just go to the nearby mall. I'm just dying to talk to you again."

And so we agreed to meet Saturday at the mall. When I hung up I found myself grinning at the phone, feeling terribly excited, as if I were planning a revolution. The first thing I did was take out my journal.

Keeping my journal up to date hadn't been at all hard. I liked the chance to tell Otero what I really thought and felt. He collected the journals once a week and commented on them.

Last week I'd written, "Power corrupts. I realize that because now I'm a Blue I could get back at Juan for throwing me in the pool and he knows it. He slinks around, avoiding me, and it hurts. We used to be such good friends, laugh together so much! How could he think I'd use my power *now* to hurt him? Yet I see other Blues taking advantage of former friends and actually seeming to enjoy it."

Otero liked that entry. He'd written, "Good insight. You're starting to grow with this experience."

Since the third day of the game we'd really separated into our color groups. Even our lunch crowd. We no longer sat together because G4's were constantly harassing Justin and Adam just because I was sitting with them. Now Justin sat with a group of his regular friends, and other Light Greens. They whispered and laughed a lot together while Adam's Orange friends seemed angry and grim most of the time. I could see why; they hardly got time to eat because someone was always coming by and expecting them to bow or do something for them. I didn't know how Adam stood it!

1 **conscience** ['kɒnʃəns] sense of what is right and wrong *(Gewissen)* – 2 **shoot!** *(AE)* expression of annoyance – 6 **ridiculous** absurd – 9 **daring** willing to take a risk – 12 **to hang up (hung, hung)** to replace the receiver on the phone – 21 **to slink around** to move about slowly and quietly as if ashamed – 25 **entry** s.th. written in a diary, dictionary, etc. – 32 **grim** feeling depressed, cheerless

Lately I sat mostly with Blues – Paul and Gwen, Raúl and Tony. Not always, but at least one or two of them seemed to join me each lunchtime. When I said how rotten I felt having friends bow to me they laughed me down.

"It's only a game, girl," Paul said. "That's the way it's supposed to be, so just play it. How will those rich dudes know what oppression's like if we don't play our part?"

"But that's not the way I'd be if I really was an upper-class person."

"Yeah? You think so?" Raúl answered. "I just bet."

"Let's sabotage the game," I suggested to the whole group one day. "Put up signs – ALL COLORS UNITE! – and see what happens. Maybe there's a whole bunch of us who'd secretly like to show Otero that society really isn't the way he's set us up."

"But it is," Gwen pointed out. She's a big-boned girl who wears her hair in little braids laced with beads. "Men don't understand women, and they don't even try. They don't have to. They have the power. And it's the same with white people. Whites don't feel they need to understand blacks. Yet *my* survival rests on understanding whites."

"That's just it," I said. "As long as there is this power difference, men won't be interested in understanding women and whites won't care about understanding any other race."

"You're getting too deep for me, Amy," Paul said. "All I see is what is ... and what is, is that nobody gives a darn about this black boy and what he thinks. Gets so I don't even care anymore. When you have nothing you have nothing much to lose."

No one at the table even blinked an eye at what Paul had said, so I guess they agreed. "Can't we change things so you won't feel that way?" I asked timidly. "I mean, if we all got together and refused to let the G4's harass the lower colors we'd be doing *some*thing."

Paul laughed and put a hand on mine. "Amy, girl. You're a good kid, but you're just one and that's not enough, see. As for me, I like things just like they are. I feel so good 'bout myself these days that even my English teacher noticed. She said, 'Paul Thomas, what got into you? You've been quiet as a mouse all term and all of a sudden

3 **rotten** miserable, terrible – 6 **dude** *(AE slang)* person, fellow, guy – 12 **bunch** group – 13 **to set s.o. up** to arrange – 15 **braid** *Haarflechte* – **laced** *here:* held with strings of beads *(Perlen)* – 23 **darn** polite way of saying "damn" – 24 **gets so** *(slang)* it gets so bad that – 26 **to blink an eye** *here:* to show any obvious reaction – 28 **timid** lacking courage, afraid – 34 **term** period of time into which a school year is divided

you've got opinions.' For the first time I got an A in an oral report. Being Blue makes me *feel* like someone."

Paul's intense, honest gaze held me for a long moment and I realized that, for him, the Color Game could go on forever, as long as he was a Blue. I turned to the others. "Do you all feel that way?"

"You're just sore 'cause you can't play with that rich white dude," Paul said, winking and nudging me. "How 'bout comin' out with this boss man? We equals now, you know," he said, using black jive.

I smiled and looked to the others. Raúl crushed a crumb with his finger. Gwen was the only one who gave me any real answer. "We got it made, being Blue. No one bothers us. We don't have to bow to anyone. We can talk to whoever we like and they gotta pay attention. We've got respect. Even the tests Ray gives us seem easy. We're getting better grades than the Oranges. Why rock the boat?" She patted my arm. "Just relax and enjoy your power, Amy, honey. It'll all be back to normal in a couple more weeks."

I stopped to visit Sue and Hideo before going to the mall to meet Carol on Saturday. Hideo was vacuuming while Sue ran a wash. "How come you're such a liberated male?" I teased my brother above the vacuum roar. "Where'd you learn it from? Papa?"

Hideo grinned and picked some papers off the floor before running the sweeper under them. He held the papers in one hand, uncertain where to put them, and finally dropped them back on the rug.

"Sue's not gonna like that," I chided.

"Oh, no?" He turned off the vacuum and pretended to chase me. I scooted between chairs and into the kitchen and from there to the bedroom and finally hid in the bathroom, where he caught me and started tickling.

"What's going on here?" Sue asked. She leaned against the doorframe, a load of clothes on her arm, trying to look severe. "Is my husband molesting you, Amy?"

3 **gaze** steady look – 6 **sore** *(AE)* hurt and angry – 7 **to wink** to quickly shut and open one's eye to show one is not serious – **how 'bout** *(slang)* how about – 8 **boss man** *(Black slang)* person in an important position – **we equals** *(Black slang)* we are equals – 9 **crumb** [krʌm] very small piece of cake or bread that has fallen off – 14 **to rock the boat** to do s.th. that changes the situation – **to pat** to hit lightly – 18 **to run a wash** *(AE)* to wash clothes in the washing-machine – 20 **roar** [rɔ:] loud deep sound – 22 **sweeper** the brush section of a vacuum cleaner – 23 **rug** *(AE)* carpet – 24 **to chide** to speak to s.o. severely for having done s.th. wrong – 28 **to tickle** *kitzeln* – 31 **to molest** [mə'lest] *here:* to annoy *(belästigen)*

Giggling, I nodded, while trying to escape Hideo's fingers. Tickling fights had been part of our fun since I was a little girl. Mama would stand by and protest mildly but she really seemed to appreciate the fun. At some point, though, Papa said it was improper for a young lady and put a stop to it.

"Okay, you two. Enough," Sue said. "I've got a pot of coffee brewing and some fresh cinnamon buns. If you can pretend to be grown-ups for a minute, join me."

We sat at the card table in the tiny kitchen eating rolls and drinking coffee and talking and laughing. I thought again how good Hideo and Sue were together.

"Did the fact that Hideo isn't the same color as you ever matter?" I asked Sue.

"Never." She licked a sugar strand from one finger. "What first attracted me was his intelligence and kindness and that quiet strength, and ..."

"Oh, Sue, come *on,*" Hideo protested, laughing. "You know that's not true. The first thing you thought was 'What a hunk!'"

Sue suppressed a grin and squinted thoughtfully at my brother. "If I'd noticed your looks first, you'd never have had a chance."

Hideo hugged her.

"Sue, really. Didn't it mean *anything* that we were Japanese?"

"Well, yes, come to think of it, it did. I was worried that he'd notice I was white ... and that it would matter to him."

"Hideo? Did it?" I hadn't known about Sue until Hideo married. He kept her such a secret, and because he was away at college, we never guessed.

Hideo's face turned serious. "Yes, it did. I tried very hard not to love Sue, knowing what it would mean to Papa and Mama. For a while I even broke it off, using some flimsy excuse ... working too hard, or something. But it didn't help. She was on my mind, in my heart, in my blood, every minute of the day and night."

"And he in mine," Sue said softly. "The brightness went out of the day when I couldn't see him."

"I thought about it a lot," Hideo said, serious eyes on mine. "I believe in tradition. It adds meaning and richness to life. Going against

6 **to brew** [bru:] to make tea, coffee, etc. with boiling water – 7 **cinnamon** *Zimt* – **bun** small round sweet bread roll – 14 **strand** thin piece of s.th. – 18 **hunk** big attractive man – 19 **to suppress** to prevent from being seen – **to squint** to look with half-closed eyes – 21 **to hug** to put one's arms around s.o. as a sign of love – 30 **flimsy** not convincing

Papa meant breaking with tradition, a frightening and enormous step to take. I didn't want to hurt the family; I didn't. But the fact is, I'm a different generation from Papa, with different history and different attitudes. I'm not afraid like he is."

"Afraid?"

"Yes. That stuff Papa carries inside him about how the Japanese-Americans were treated during World War II is *his* poison, not mine. I can't let it warp how I feel. It's made him fear 'outsiders', anyone who isn't Japanese. And it's time he got over that."

Sue put a hand on Hideo's. I guess she knew about the internment camps, about our family's life there, something we didn't speak about even to each other.

"Under the skin people all want the same ... food on the table, a good job, a family to love, peace in the world. What's color got to do with it?" Hideo asked.

"Color does, darling," Sue said. "It's so much harder to make it when you're not white. It's possible, sure, but prejudice runs deep. Maybe that's what this game Amy's playing at school is all about. Maybe those kids will go away realizing how much prejudice hurts and they'll judge people for what they are, not by their color or class."

When I left Sue and Hideo to meet Carol, my head swarmed with things to think about. Despite what Hideo said, I wanted to show Otero we shouldn't treat each other so badly. I could hardly wait to tell Carol about some of my ideas.

We met, as usual, in front of the mall bookstore. Carol arrived early. She was already at the checkout, paying for some books.

"Look," Carol slipped three books out of the bag and fanned them out for me to see. Each had a typical romance cover, a girl and two boys, or two girls and one boy. Carol buys all the new titles when they come out each month and insists on telling me what's in them.

She frowned this time as she put them away. "I never noticed before, but they never show a black or Latino girl on these covers – or Asian. Don't they think we fall in love, too?"

Arm in arm we wandered through the mall, which was mobbed

8 **to warp** to twist; to influence in a bad way – 10 **internment camp** a prison-like camp usually for political prisoners as used for Japanese and Japanese-Americans during World War Two – 26 **checkout** place where one pays in a shop – 27 **to fan out** to spread out in a half circle like a fan *(Fächer)* – 34 **mobbed** very crowded

with shoppers. Usually, half the kids in school hang out there Saturdays, mostly looking each other over. That's how I met Adam. Last summer I was a salesgirl at the Toy Factory and he came in to buy something for Bettina's birthday. I caught him watching me while I served three customers and when he finally asked my help, he had me completely flustered. Just thinking of him now made me glow.

"You left your armband *home*, right?" I asked Carol as we headed for the fast-food section.

"Yeah, well, not exactly." She gave me a sheepish grin. "At the last minute ... I ..." She held her arm out with its dark-green band. "I figured you'd probably bring yours."

"Well, I didn't. Not my journal, either."

Carol stopped short, so that a woman pushing a stroller bumped into her. "I'm sorry. What do you want to do? I don't want to get you in trouble. We can eat somewhere else."

A feeling of excitement, not unlike fear, raced through me. Without my journal and band I felt almost naked. "No, no. It doesn't matter. In fact that's what I wanted to talk to you about."

"Let's get out of here. This place is too public."

We turned away from the colored tables and stools in the center of the food concessions and went to McDonald's. There we settled down with Big Macs and colas in a back booth. I breathed a sigh of relief when it appeared that we were the only members of Otero's class there.

"Juan's coming over tonight," Carol said, scraping onions off her burger. "We're having an engagement party for my brother and Laura." She licked a finger, then took a bite of her Big Mac. Mouth full, she added, "Laura doesn't know it yet, but when she marries my brother and changes her name to Rodriguez, it's gonna be a whole new ball game."

I nodded. "She knows, but if they love each other, they'll survive. Look at Hideo and Sue. I think Otero's game means to exaggerate. Just look how he's set us off against each other. How can you even go with Juan, when he's a Light Green?"

1 **to hang out** *(AE)* to spend a lot of time somewhere – 6 **flustered** nervous and confused – **to glow** to feel happy – 13 **stroller** ['strəʊlə] *(AE)* pushchair *(BE)* *Kinderwagen* – **to bump into s.o.** to hit or knock against s.o. – 21**concession** *(AE)* restaurant or service within s.o. else's shop – 22 **booth** [bu:θ] enclosed place in a restaurant with a table and long seats – 25 **to scrape off** to remove with a sharp insturment – **onion** ['ʌnɪən] *Zwiebel* – 26 **engagement** the act of promising to marry s.o. – 30 **ball game** *(AE) here:* situation, set of rules

Carol gave me a lopsided grin. "Where Juan's concerned, nothing can come between us. We're too close. Except," she said, more seriously, "in school. There I expect him to treat me with the respect lower colors should show to their superiors!"

"Carol ..."

She giggled. "I'm just playing Otero's game ... that's all ... just going by the rules."

"Why don't we unite ... rebel against this dumb game and show Otero that people don't have to do what he expects them to?"

Carol gave me a suspicious glance. "What's this? Since when have you become an activist?"

"I'm not!"

Carol ran her tongue around the ends of the Big Mac. "Anyway, what could we do?"

"Stop wearing our bands. Bow back to those lower than us. Ignore his rules and talk to anyone we want to, no matter what color."

"Whoops," Carol warned with a nod of her head. "G4."

"Well, hello, you two," Brian said, smiling down at me. "Enjoying yourselves?"

With a kind of glee Carol raised her right arm and showed off her band. "See, I've got it. Want to see my journal, too? Have it right here."

Brian continued to smile at me as Carol dug into her bag and triumphantly drew out the notebook.

Some perverse stubbornness in me wanted Brian to notice my missing color band. So I folded my hands very obviously on top of the table. I'd been chided by other G4's any number of times about this or that wrong. But when punishments were given out in class, somehow I never suffered. I was beginning to think it was deliberate. Maybe Otero had a reason to keep me a Blue.

Brian riffled through the pages of Carol's journal to the entry dated the day before. "Let's see. ..." He started reading. " '... I panicked when I couldn't find my armband. How could I go to school without it? I thought of making a new band, or tying a green scarf around ... anything so I'd not be demoted!' " Brian said, "You would have been, too!" He read on. " 'Today I saw Adam. Even though he's Amy's

1 **lopsided** *here:* with her head leaning to one side – 17 **whoops!** [wʊps] *Hoppla!* – **nod** slight downward movement of the head as a sign – 20 **glee** joy – 25 **stubbornness** the quality of being very strong-willed, refusing to change a decision made – 27 **any number of times** many times – 29 **deliberate** done on purpose – 31 **to riffle** ['rɪfl] **through** to turn the pages quickly

boyfriend, I've never quite liked him. He makes me feel like I'm not good enough for him.' "

Carol's face flushed pink and I couldn't look at her.

" 'I expected Adam to bow, naturally,' " Brian continued. " 'He laughed at me and said, 'Ah, C'mon, Carol.' That made me really angry. I thought he was refusing because of my friendship with Amy and maybe because I'm Chicana. How dare he, the lowest of the low, not show proper respect? I made him bow again! Later, I felt ashamed and confused. In the beginning it was fun getting people to bow. Now, I don't know.' "

Brian closed the book and handed it back to Carol. "How come you're socializing with Amy? You know the rules."

"Oh, yeah? How come you're after me?" Carol cried. "Amy doesn't even have her armband or journal with her and I don't see you –" Carol clapped her hands over her mouth and looked at me in horror.

"Is that true, Amy?"

"Uh-huh." I held my arm up to prove it.

"Of course you forgot. These things happen."

With pounding heart and wet palms I said, "No, I didn't forget. I decided not to wear it, or to bring my journal, either."

Brian's eyebrows went up. "May I ask why?"

"Because I don't believe that being a particular color makes you any better than anyone else."

"That's treason, you know."

"I guess so."

"You realize what you're forcing me to do?"

"You'll have to report me."

Brian sighed and shook his head. He tugged a small spiral notebook from his back jeans pocket. "Either one of you got a pencil?" he asked, embarrassed.

I smiled. With trembling fingers I pulled a ballpoint out of my purse and handed it to him. He nodded, and without so much as a thanks, wrote down my name and my terrible, treasonous act.

7 **Chicana** [tʃɪ'kɑ:na] female Mexican-American – 13 **to be after s.o.** to want to catch s.o. in order to punish them – 15 **to clap** to place an open hand on s.th. – 19 **palm** [pɑ:m] the inside part of the hand not including the fingers – 24 **treason** ['tri:zn] disloyalty *(Verrat)* – 31 **ballpoint** ballpoint pen, biro – **purse** *(AE)* woman's handbag

Chapter 8

The way I figured, by Monday I'd be an Orange.

Why couldn't I accept being a Blue like the others and play out Otero's game the way he'd set it up? Why think mutiny when I'd never in my life opposed anything if it meant bringing attention to myself or being in disfavor?

Another thing. How could I, the superachiever, resist earning the most points by oppressing others so I'd win the prize when the class ended? It didn't make much sense, yet the thought of resistance grew and grew in me like a tumor you couldn't control.

Adam was away at his family's mountain home helping get it ready for the ski season, so I couldn't talk it out with him. We wouldn't see each other until Monday. I knew he'd be gone, but Bettina told me something Adam hadn't.

"I passed the math test!" she cried, first thing, when she phoned Friday. "Isn't that super?"

"Wonderful! What did you get?"

Her voice dropped, but only for an instant. "Sixty-nine." Then she hurried on, excited again. "Mama says you're to come back next week and tutor me some more." Before I could digest that order, told so bluntly, she added, "We're leaving any minute on our trip to the mountains so I'll have to run. But did you know about that big party Adam's having Saturday night?"

"Party?" My mind lingered on the way Bettina gave me her mother's news.

"I bet Adam didn't tell you. He's got gobs of friends coming to stay over."

Adam had invited friends for the weekend? Surprised and hurt that he'd said nothing to me, that I hadn't been invited, I didn't answer.

"Aren't you going to ask who's coming?" Bettina persisted.

"I have the feeling you'll tell me anyway," I said.

Bettina giggled and I could almost see her counting off the names on her fingers. "There's Melissa and Justin, Eileen and Beth ..."

1 **to figure** *(AE)* to believe, to calculate – 3 **mutiny** ['mju:tɪnɪ] rebellion (especially among sailors or soldiers) – 5 **disfavor** (*BE* disfavour) being disliked or disapproved of – 6 **superachiever** extremely competent student – 7 **class** i.e. course – 17 **sixty-nine** i. e. 69% of the test was correct (not a good result) – 19 **to digest** ['dɪdʒest] *here:* to take in *(verdauen)* – 20 **blunt** direct, not trying to be polite –23 **to linger** ['lɪŋgə] to stay with s.th. for a while – 25 **gobs** *(AE slang)* lots – 29 **to persist** to continue in a determined way

Eileen? She was the girl Mrs. Tarcher always pushed at Adam. Pretty, bright, from one of the best families, she was so much better suited to him than I. Why was she at his party, *staying over,* and not me?

When I hung up, I didn't want to admit how puzzled and betrayed Bettina's news left me. And the feelings remained. On Saturday, as I toyed with thoughts of rebellion, I not only couldn't talk it out with Adam, but I wouldn't even have wanted to, had he been in town. Yet I had so much need to sort out my plans with someone, to hear that my instincts were right. That it wouldn't be a mistake to give up all the power of being a Blue for the nebulous hope that I could change things as an Orange.

I guess, out of this need, I turned to my father, even knowing in advance how he'd likely answer.

We were huddled together opposite each other at the chessboard in the living room Saturday night. I'd told him bits and pieces about the Color Game and my thoughts between plays. The weather had turned cold and it felt good to be indoors where it was bright and warm. The house smelled of Mama's baking, pumpkin and apple pies for Thanksgiving dinner. She was getting ready for the big family gathering when all of us, Grandma and Grandpa, aunts, uncles, cousins, and this year Sue and Hideo, were together.

"So what do you think, Papa?" I asked. I'd just lost my bishop to his knight, something that wouldn't have happened if I'd paid better attention. Papa shook his head in dismay, folded his arms across his chest, and stared at me.

"When I play chess I like to concentrate, not talk," he said.

"I know, Papa. But this Color Game is important to me and I can't concentrate on chess because all I can think about is what I should do."

"All right." Papa leaned back and studied me. "But first I have to ask, are you being honest with yourself? Are you wanting to give up being a Blue just for that ... boy ... to be with him?"

"Oh, Papa," I cried. "No!"

"Good. Then I ask, what can you accomplish by losing all that

2 **bright** intelligent – 3 **suited** suitable – 5 **betrayed** treated disloyally – 11 **nebulous** ['nebjʊləs] vague, unclear – 15 **to be huddled** to be crowded together – **chessboard** *Schachbrett* – 17 **play** *here: Zug* – 19 **pumpkin** large round orange vegetable *(Kürbis)* – 20 **gathering** coming together of people – 23 **bishop** *Läufer (Schach)* – 24 **knight** [naɪt] *Springer (Schach)* – 25 **dismay** feeling of anxiety and hopelessness – 35 **to accomplish** to succeed in doing

status? You become a social outcast. You'd have all those ... what do you call them ... G4's ... down on you."

"Yes. But maybe, with Adam's help, we can organize the Oranges and Light Greens and get some improvement in the way we're treated."

"It is better, because of who you are, to work hard and be a good citizen and not get into trouble. When you protest, you start trouble." He hesitated, then added, "When I was a boy in the camp they sent us to, it was very bad. We were called 'yellow devils.' We were 'inscrutable.' You know what that means?"

I thought of Adam's note with the flowers. He had called me "exotic" and "inscrutable." I had considered it a compliment, meaning *mysterious.*

"In those days the word meant *sly, sneaky.* Such shame, to call us that!" Papa shook his head in distress, then went on. "My father tried to change things. People listened to him. But the authorities got worried. They didn't want trouble. They sent him to another camp, away from us!"

I'd heard that story and others like it all my life and they always left me feeling insecure. What happened to Papa was a long time ago. Times have changed. I want to believe people wouldn't let that happen again.

"Papa?" I asked. "If Grandma and Grandpa's *hakujin* friends had protested to the government during those days, maybe all our people wouldn't have been put away for those years."

"Ahh!" Papa said with distaste. "I don't want to talk about it!"

"Why? Please, Papa, think about it. Wouldn't it have changed things?"

"It wouldn't have made a difference. We were treated badly because we *looked* different. The Germans in America were just as much a threat, but they weren't sent away. They didn't *look* different, that's why."

"Hideo and Sue think I should do what I think is right, not what's safe."

"Hideo ... Hideo and Sue ... ach! What do they know? My son has

1 **outcast** s.o. driven away from friends, society, etc. – 2 **to be down on s.o.** to want to make s.o. miserable – 8 **the camp** i. e. the internment camp during World War Two – 14 **sly** [slaɪ] dishonestly tricky – **sneaky** acting secretly in order to trick others – 15 **distress** suffering of the mind – 20 **insecure** anxious and unsure of oneself – 23 **hakujin** white – 26 **distaste** a strong feeling of dislike – 31 **threat** [θret] *here:* danger

gone to college and he has married a white girl, so he thinks he knows everything." With more than a trace of bitterness Papa added, "I have lived much longer than your brother. What I know is from experience. What I say is right." With that Papa returned his attention to the chess set.

Papa's reaction helped me decide. Being cautious, being safe, never changed anything. Hideo was right. Papa lived too much in the past, was filled too much with old fears. I was a *sansei,* a third generation, as was Hideo. While we didn't want to lose our traditions, our strong sense of the past, we couldn't let our parents' old ways and old fears and suspicions taint us.

I spent much of Sunday in my room, lettering the posters. ALL COLORS UNITE, each board read. I'd printed the word UNITE in the four colors of the game. It was an odd feeling, quite unfamiliar, to plot by myself what I'd do, knowing the consequences. All day I buzzed with a kind of happy zeal.

While working on the posters I considered how I'd put them up. It would be impossible to mount them on walls during school hours without being seen and without the G4's taking them down immediately. They had to be put up before Monday so they'd be there for everyone to see, first thing. But how?

Juan. His name came to me instantly. Juan would enjoy the adventure. It was exactly the kind of thing he'd go for without a second's hesitation.

"We'll do it tonight," he said when I phoned, delighted with the idea. "There's a night watchman, so we'll have to be careful. Wear sneakers and jeans. Pick you up at eight."

I felt scared and exhilarated as I climbed the chain link fence and dropped down to the school grounds. Juan followed, first throwing me the bundle of banners and posters. Then together we ran toward

6 **cautious** ['kɔ:ʃəs] being careful to avoid risks – 11 **suspicions** feeling that you cannot trust others *(Misstrauen)* – **to taint** to affect in a negative way, to spoil – 14 **to plot** to make a secret plan to do s.th. – 16 **zeal** [zi:l] eagerness, enthusiasm – 18 **to mount** to fix – 24 **hesitation** act of taking a pause before acting – 27 **sneakers** ['sni:kəz] *(AE)* light shoes made of cloth used for sports – 28 **exhilarated** joyously excited – **chain link fence** fence made of metal wires formed into links *(Kettenglied)* to prevent people from getting through – 30 **banner** a piece of cloth on which s.th. is written, often held between two poles

the gym, the first place we planned to post, giggling with suppressed excitement.

We hung the signs one by one, at the library, outside the cafeteria, next to the johns, wherever kids would see them. We slunk down halls, peered around corners, whispered and pointed like criminals robbing a bank. *It was so easy,* we couldn't believe it! And finally, there was only one more place to hang a sign, on the notice board right beside the front office.

"There's a light on!" I whispered, stopping in my tracks some feet from the door.

"I'll look." Juan moved swiftly and silently, then scrunched down to peer through the glass which covered the upper half of the door. He nodded, then motioned for me to come. Heart pounding, I tiptoed to him, bent, and peeked into the room. The night watchman was seated at a desk, feet up, munching a sandwich and watching a small TV set. "Piece of cake," Juan whispered as we grinned at each other.

Cool as you please, we taped the last ALL COLORS UNITE sign right there, on the glass. Then, hand in hand and giggling, we fled back to the fence, climbed its links, and dropped down to the street, where we ran off like criminals. When we reached my house we went over every step of what we'd done, praising each other for how well it had gone.

As he said good-night, Juan gave me a quick hug, then pumped my hand vigorously. "We done good, pardner," he said, grinning.

"We sure did!" I reached up and kissed him on the cheek.

It would have been perfect if Adam had phoned so I could tell him what we'd done and get his reactions. But Adam's weekend must have gone on longer than planned, because he didn't call. I tried not to let myself dwell on it or the disappointment would take away my wonderful high..

I left for school early the next day wearing my armband like a good Blue. The first Color Game student I met was Gia, a Light Green. Glancing first at my band, then my face, she bowed. I bowed back. Puzzled, she looked again at my band and bowed a second time. Smiling, I returned the bow. Not quite sure what to make of me she

1 **gym** [dʒɪm] gymnasium *(Turnhalle)* – **to post** to place s.th. in a certain position – **suppressed** not shown openly – 4 **john** *(AE slang)* toilet – **to slink, slunk, slunk** to move quietly so as not to be seen – 9 **in one's tracks** suddenly – 11 **to scrunch down** to lower the body by bending the legs together – 16 **piece of cake** an easy task to perform – 17 **to tape** mit Klebeband befestigen – 23 **vigorously** energetically – **done good** *(AE slang)* have done well – **pardner** partner – 28 **to dwell on s.th.** to think about s.th. for a long time

fell in step behind as inferior colors are supposed to do. I stopped and faced her. "Gia, this is pretty silly. Why don't we walk together?"

Gia looked around to see who might be watching. "You mean it?"

"Sure, why not?"

"Oh, come on! I'll just get reported, not you." She stepped back. "Thanks, but no thanks."

I shrugged and walked on. Whenever a lower color bowed to me I bowed back. Mostly I got puzzled and surprised looks, but no one asked "how come?" I wondered who, if any of them, would be first to report me to earn Otero's precious points.

Everyone in school was talking about the mysterious signs and banners that had bloomed overnight. Who had dared put them there? Was a revolution in the making? How would the power structure react?

As I passed the main office, two Dark Greens were directing Oranges to strip the poster from the glass door and pull down the banner spanning the second-floor balconies. "How dare those uppity lower classes do that!" one of them said. I guess most people assumed it had to be Oranges who had put them up.

All through morning classes my mind was busy elsewhere. What would happen in Otero's class? Couldn't everyone tell, by the way I looked, how guilty I was?

At lunchtime I took one more step toward demotion. Instead of sitting with the Blues, I joined Juan at the Light Green table. At first the kids said, "Please, go away. You'll just get us in trouble." But when Juan whispered about our Sunday night escapade, there were so many questions and so much laughter that people started turning around to look our way. Of course the G4's noticed, and pretty soon there was Brian behind me.

"Aren't you at the wrong table, Amy? What are you doing, slumming?"

"Oh, hi, Brian!" I smiled brightly at him, while my heart pounded in my ears. "Why don't you join us? We're talking about the posters all over school – you know, ALL COLORS UNITE?"

"Those posters are revolutionary. Whoever put them up will be severely punished."

10 **precious** ['preʃəs] of great value, worth a lot – 12 **to bloom** to appear in great numbers – 16 **to strip** to remove, to take off from s.th. – 17 **to span** to stretch across – 18 **to assume** to accept as true before there is any proof – 26 **escapade** ['eskəpeɪd] daring or exciting act – 30 **to slum** to visit a place that is lower than one's own social class just for the fun of it

Juan was trying hard to keep a straight face. One or two Light Greens chortled quietly, covering their mouths to hide their amusement.

"Am I missing something?" Brian asked. "Do you know something I don't? Was it the Light Greens, perhaps, and not the Oranges who are to blame? Because if anyone knows, there'll be a big reward in points for telling."

"Us rebel? We wouldn't think of it!" Juan cried in mock horror. "Light Greens are good fellows. All we want is to keep what we've got and not cause trouble!"

"You realize, I hope," Brian said sternly, "That inferior colors should not be conversing with their superiors."

"Oh, that's all right, Brian," I said. "They're not talking to me. I'm talking to them."

Brian didn't quite know what to make of us. Most of the kids studiously avoided looking at him while seeming to be holding back giggles. After an uncomfortable silence he wrote something in his notebook, frowned, and went away.

"Hey, girl," Paul Thomas said in greeting as soon as I took my seat in Otero's class, "I've been hearing things. What're you up to, anyway?"

I turned around to face him, glancing first at the back of the room where Adam sat talking with an Orange. We hadn't said a word to each other since Friday. "Depends on what you heard," I said, wishing Adam would look my way.

"Baaad things ... real baaad," Paul said. He leaned forward confidentially. "Seems you've been bowing to all the lowlife. You've been sitting with Light Greens. ..."

I smiled. "They're my friends, Paul. Some were my friends before this game and just because some stupid law says they're not anymore, doesn't mean I'll obey it."

Gwen, seated beside me, tuned in. Her face took on the look of someone who has smelled something bad. She edged away.

The class began before we could talk any longer, and after roll call Otero started in on the book we were supposed to have read, *Black*

2 **to chortle** to laugh with pleasure – 11 **sternly** severely, seriously – 12 **to converse with s.o.** to talk with s.o. – 15 **studiously** with great care – 25 **confidentially** said so that not everyone should hear what he's saying – 26 **lowlife** people of the lower classes – 31 **to tune in** *(slang)* to realize the importance of what is being said – 32 **to edge away** to move away slowly – 33 **roll call** reading the list of names to see who is present

Like Me. It deals with a white man, a well-known writer named Griffin, an educated man with a nice family. He decided to find out if *color* really made a difference in how people were treated. So, he dyed his skin by taking some special medicine and went to live as a black man in the South. What he discovered was that everything changed, just because he was black. People didn't care that he was an educated man, well-bred, decent, a published author. All they saw was that he was *black.* He had to sit in the back of buses and walk for miles sometimes to find a toilet he'd be allowed to use, or a restaurant that would serve him. The book was written maybe twenty years ago, and things are better now, Otero says, but blacks still aren't treated like first-class citizens.

Paul said, "It's good that a white dude wrote the book, because no one would believe what it's like if a black man said those things."

Justin said, "People *always* want to be superior to others. Look how that black shoeshine guy abused the wino. There's a pecking order, no matter what color you are."

I wasn't so sure about that because I remembered the shoeshine man in the book *did* put some food aside for the wino. But I didn't say anything. Frankly, I was so scared about what would happen when the G4's took over, as they did each class period, that I couldn't concentrate.

And finally, it began. Otero turned the class over to Brian that day to handle the fines and awards.

You could actually feel the tension in the class, mostly in the back rows, because they could always expect the worst treatment. My color and the Dark Greens could sit back and just watch the show.

"IRS refunds have just come in," Brian began. 'The following people please come up to get your checks: Tony, Gwen ... Gia, Mark ..." Except for Gia, all the names called belonged in the higher colors. "Carol, we've had some very good reports on you and have decided to promote you to Blue."

I glanced back at Carol and smiled. Carol hurried forward and Mary pinned a Blue armband over the Dark Green. Then she took a seat beside me.

3 **to dye** [daɪ] to give a different color – 7 **well-bred** having been taught good manners – 16 **shoeshine guy** person who shines people's shoes – **to abuse** [ə'bju:z] to treat badly – **wino** an alcoholic who drinks wine – **pecking order** *Hackordnung* – 24 **award** a prize or money – 28 **IRS** Internal Revenue Service in the U.S.A., the government agency that collects taxes – **refund** ['ri:fʌnd] money given back

"Several people have been fined for late payment of income tax. Ten-dollar fines for Cynthia, Adam, Bob ..." This time most of those fined were lower colors. A couple more fines were given, sometimes unjustly, and awards, sometimes without being honestly earned, then Brian said:

"It has come to our attention that the people responsible for putting up the signs on campus are the Oranges. Would those involved please stand up, or else the entire Orange class will have to bear the consequences."

Everyone turned around to see what the Oranges would do. Adam leaned forward, an intense, angry scowl on his face. Others looked startled, guarded, even scared. Of course no one admitted blame. I felt hot with guilt, shocked that someone else might take blame for what I'd done.

"You all realize, don't you, that the state will not tolerate troublemakers," Brian said. "You lower colors have as much opportunity to rise in society as anyone else. If you don't make it, you have only yourselves to blame. Nobody's going to give up their good lives just because you're not ambitious enough to get where *they* are." His face hardened. "Now, don't hurt your own people, whoever you are. Stand up and admit your guilt and take your punishment. If the guilty person or persons do not stand up –"

I jumped to my feet. With the attention centered on the Oranges in the back of the room, no one noticed me at first. Then Brian said, "Amy, sit down."

"*I'm* responsible for the posters and banners," I said. My face must have turned scarlet from the way it burned and the words came out as if I'd just finished running. The room became so still I could hear Gwen gasp, and all eyes fixed on me. "Sunday night I climbed the fence and put up the signs."

Brian's lips curled into a curious smile. "You did, did you? If that's true, you're in real trouble, Amy. But I can't believe it. It's too big a job for one person. Who helped you?"

"Nobody. I did it alone." My face burned and I carefully avoided looking at Juan.

"No, she didn't!" Juan's chair scraped as he leaped to his feet. "I helped her!"

8 **to bear** to take, to accept – 11 **scowl** [skaʊl] expression of anger on the face – 12 **startled** shocked and frightened – **guarded** careful not to show one's feelings – 27 **scarlet** bright red – 29 **to gasp** to breathe in suddenly because of surprise – 36 **to scrape** to rub roughly against a surface

"I see." Brian's eyebrows rose in surprise. He glanced first at Otero, then at the other G4's. "I'll have to confer with my colleagues for a moment." I stood before the class like Hester Prynne before the townspeople, while Juan and I gazed uneasily at each other. Brian, Otero, and the other G4's whispered for a while, then Brian stepped back to the front of the room.

"We're very disappointed in you, Amy. Very. Reports have come in that you've been urging others to rebel, that you've been bowing back to lower colors. That you've deliberately left your own color and conspired with lower colors. And now you admit to an even worse crime – insurrection." Brian shook his head. "Of course you know you've disgraced your color. No one of status will want to have anything to do with you. And because of the severity of your crimes and your unrepentant attitude, we have no choice but to demote you to the lowest status. From now on you are ... an Orange. Of course you keep your blue band on under the orange, because it symbolizes your roots."

I let out my breath, relieved to have it over with. Others had been promoted and demoted, but never more than one level higher or lower. It was so embarrassing. It's what I'd expected to happen, even wanted to happen. But now that it had, I felt so strange. My entire upbringing had taught me to bring respect and honor to the family name and my own, and to do it without bringing attention to myself. Papa would be so ashamed.

Still, I didn't feel disgraced. Embarrassed, yes, even a little scared. I gathered up my books and walked with head high to the G4 holding the color bands. With everyone watching, I proudly wrapped the orange band on top of the blue. As I walked to the back of the room I heard Brian shouting at Juan. "You're so stupid, you might just as well be an Orange, too!"

"Way to go!" someone whispered as I passed the Light Greens. Hands reached out to touch me. Ahead, in the Orange section, sat a

2 **to confer** to talk with others for advice – 3 **Hester Prynne** [prɪn] a character in the novel *The Scarlet Letter* by the American author Nathaniel Hawthorne (1804-1864). She was made to feel ashamed because of an illegitimate child. – 9 **to conspire** to plan s.th. secretly with others – 11 **insurrection** open revolt against the people in power – 12 **to disgrace** to bring shame and dishonor on s.th./s.o. – 13 **unrepentant** not willing to feel sorry for having done s.th. bad – 17 **roots** where you come from – 21 **upbringing** the training a child receives while growing up – 31 **Way to go!** Well done! Bravo!

solid row of females, or Teks, with the only seat at the end. Without a word the row stood up and Teks moved right and left, leaving a seat in the middle for me. Right in front of Adam.

Adam's eyes glowed with pride and love. I took the seat in front of him and faced front, feeling oddly vulnerable. But I had no doubt that what I'd done was right.

5 **oddly** strangely

Chapter 9

"You did it for me, didn't you?" Adam asked, an arm around me as we left the room together for the first time in weeks. "So we could be together. Despite everything you said, you just couldn't stand being away from me, right?"

Part of me remained tied up in knots at what I'd done and part of me wanted to stay aloof from Adam, not wanting to be hurt after what Bettina had said. But looking up at his handsome, confident face, I couldn't stay angry. Instead, I smiled and said, "Actually, I did it for me."

Juan fell into step beside us. "Did she tell you how we plastered the school last night? You should have seen her climb that fence, like a commando. Cool as a killer. Man! I never knew you had that side to you, Amy."

"Oh, come on," I chided. "If you hadn't agreed to come, I'd never have had the guts. We had fun, though, didn't we?" Our escapade had created a special bond of affection between us. Adam noticed, and turned silent and aloof. I went on chatting with Juan, hoping Adam would get over his rudeness, until Juan left us at the stairs.

For the next moments Adam and I walked together without speaking. Finally, I said, "What's wrong?"

"You tell me!" Adam exclaimed. "What's going on between you and that ... macho Mex?"

"Adam!" I couldn't believe what I heard.

"What's with you, Amy? Since when do you call on Juan? How come you didn't phone me to go with you?"

"I don't see where it's your right to tell me who to see or not! Did I say you shouldn't go to the beach because all those girls would be around? And anyway, you were up in the mountains, *as I recall!*" Pride wouldn't let me add, "With your real friends."

"You could have waited a day!"

3 **despite** in spite of – 5 **knot** [nɒt] *Knoten; here:* feeling of discomfort – 6 **aloof** [ə'lu:f] distant, apart (especially in feelings) – 10 **to plaster** to cover all over – 12 **commando** specially trained soldier – 15 **guts** *(slang)* courage and determination – 16 **bond** s.th. that unites two people or groups –**affection** fondness – 17 **to chat** to talk in an informal and friendly manner – 18 **to get over** *überwinden* – **rudeness** impoliteness – 22 **macho** ['mætʃəʊ] *(Spanish)* being overly proud of being a man – **Mex** Mexican – 28 **to recall** to remember

"I'm not even sure you would have gone along with it. You're an Orange. *Aspiring to rise in Otero's magic kingdom.*"

"What's gotten into you? What's with all this sarcasm?"

"That's the second time you've asked that! Well, nothing's gotten into me. Maybe this is who I really am. Do you prefer the good old quiet, don't-make-waves me?" My throat ached and my heart pounded in my ears. Somehow I couldn't shut up that mean rush of words.

By now we'd reached my typing class and the warning bell had rung, so Adam should have been leaving for his own class. We stood in the hall staring at each other, glaring at each other really, as the last stragglers hurried by. Suddenly, all my anger drained away and I put a hand on Adam's. "Why are we arguing like this? We can be together now without all those outside pressures. There's enough meanness in the upper colors without hurting each other, too." I held out my hand with its orange armband. "I'm just a lowly Orange, just like you now. Let's not fight. Let's work together."

Adam's eyes softened and he took my hands in his.

"You're right and I'm sorry. I shouldn't have said that about Juan. Forgive me?"

"Sure."

He glanced down the hall. "I better go. But we're having an Orange meeting at my house at four. Can you be there?"

"Sure."

He nodded, turned, and strode away, blowing me a kiss before disappearing around a corner. I stood for a long moment, staring off at nothing, thinking.

How quickly I'd accepted Adam's apology about Juan, but how hard it would be to forget what he'd said. Did he really think of Juan that way? What would happen, I wondered, when he didn't like something I said or did? Would he view *me* as a "Jap" then?

As I went into the typing room I thought about his weekend. He'd said nothing about the party, about Eileen and the others, as if he owed me no explanations. Then, what right had he to question me about Juan?

Confused and troubled, I took my seat and uncovered the electric

2 **to aspire** to direct one's efforts to achieve a goal – 10 **to glare** to look at in an angry way – 11 **straggler** person who has moved away from the main group because of being too slow – **to drain away** to flow away, to disappear – 27 **apology** a statement saying one is sorry for having done s.th. bad – 30 **Jap** *(derog.)* Japanese person – 33 **to owe** [əʊ] to feel the need to do or give s.th.

typewriter. We were having a timed test. Usually, I could forget everything except what magic flowed from my eyes through my head to my fingers. Now, as I rolled a paper into the machine, all I could see was Adam and the cold, superior look he'd had on his face when he spoke about Juan.

They were meeting in the game room in back of Adam's home, a maid said as she ushered me through endless corridors to a room I'd not seen before. It was big enough to hold a hundred people comfortably, and the dozen to fifteen kids seemed lost in the huge space. Some were clustered around two large game tables, playing or kibbitzing. Others, including Adam, sat near a stone fireplace, talking and laughing. In the background I heard an old Beatles album playing.

As soon as Adam saw me he rushed forward, taking my hand and drawing me into the room. "Hey, everyone! Look who's here! The Joan of Arc of Ray Otero's class!"

"Three cheers for Amy!" someone cried as everyone gathered at the fireplace. The room rang with cheers. I covered my face in embarrassment, but not before noticing something odd. Two of Adam's friends, Troy Crichton and Dana Ellerby, hadn't joined in the cheering. They'd stood there, slightly apart, with strange, aloof, suspicious smiles on their faces.

Adam lit the wood in the stone fireplace and soon a roaring fire burned. We sat on leather chairs and sofas, or on the floor, and ate sandwiches from a silver tray. I sat on the floor, leaning against Adam's legs, and thought how very different it was from being a Blue, how very *pleasant*.

Juan arrived late, looking around as if he felt uncomfortable. He gestured at the rich surroundings, the Oriental rugs, the wall of books, the paintings. "If *this* is the life of an Orange, let me at it!"

Adam gave him a strained smile and made a space for him near us. Some of the kids tittered. Troy and Dana exchanged knowing glances.

Juan had always been forthright, but this observation made me uncomfortable. He was right, of course. If this was a gathering of *really* poor people, we'd be meeting in a church hall, or in a tiny apartment smelling of cooking and loud with the noises of too many people.

7 **to usher** to lead s.o. to a certain place – 10 **to kibbitz** *(Yiddish)* to observe and give unwanted advice – 15 **Joan of Arc** (1412–1432) French national heroine, who helped to defeat the English in the Hundred Years' War – 28 **to gesture** ['dʒestʃə] to make a movement with a part of the body to express or show s.th. – 30 **strained** tense – 31 **to titter** to laugh in a silly way – 32 **forthright** open, frank, direct

To ease the tension I said, “One nice thing about being an Orange is getting together like this. When I was a Blue, we never met after school.”

“Sure, why would you?” Troy asked with the same odd smile he’d had when I first came in. “You already had everything. Why would you give all that up?”

“Because ... because ...” I stopped, a cold chill running down my back. Would he understand that you condone a system if you don’t oppose what you don’t like?

“You act like you don’t believe we’re for real,” Juan said, reaching for another sandwich.

Dana ignored his response. Smiling sweetly, as if she didn’t mean a word of harm, she asked, “Did it ever occur to you guys that they might be spies, spies Otero planted to find out what we’re up to?” She gazed around at everyone – everyone except me.

I stiffened and Adam squeezed my shoulder comfortingly. “Come on, Dana. You always think the worst of people. Why don’t you take what Amy did at face value?”

“Yeah, sure, Dana,” one of the others offered. “We’ve got enough troubles without you putting doubts in [illegible] head about our own people.”

I kept this fixed smile on my face, trembling inside. Even though nobody really believed what Dana had said, she’d planted doubt. I huddled closer to Adam’s legs.

“We’re here to talk about what’s going on with us,” Troy said. “So, tell me how you’d handle this one. I was in the locker room yesterday getting ready for soccer practice, and this guy Paul – you know who I mean – he’s talking to some guy next to him – no one in the Color Game – and he says, loud enough for everyone to hear, ‘If a Light Green were to marry an Orange, what would their kids be like?’ ”

“Too dumb to steal,” Juan said grimly.

For a second no one laughed, then everyone did. Juan smiled.

“I don’t see what’s so funny,” Dana Ellerby said.

“I heard the same joke two months ago,” Juan said, “except it was about a Latino and a Black.”

1 **to ease** to lessen – 8 **to condone** to regard as acceptable although it is morally wrong – 10 **to be for real** *(AE)* to be serious about s.th. – 13 **to occur to s.o.** to come to s.o.’s mind – 17 **to take s.th. at face value** to accept s.th. as it seems to be *(etwas für bare Münze nehmen)* – 26 **locker room** *(AE)* room for changing clothes with lockers *(Schließfächer)* in a sports club, gymnasium, etc.

"Well, what do we do about it? Are we going to stand for these put-downs without putting up a fight? Should we maybe answer with some good jokes of our own?"

"Like what?" someone asked. "Most mean jokes like that are racist or about the poor. Is that what Otero's been trying to show, that jokes say what we really feel?"

"So what are we here for?" Troy asked. "If we can't do anything about the way we're treated, what's the good? No matter how I try, I get fined. I write in my journal every day like a good, obedient Orange and a G4 makes fun of it. I bow and curtsy until my back aches and get fined the next day for what I *didn't* do! I protest the fine and Otero makes me look stupid! What's the use of trying? They want to keep us down and they're doing it."

"Yeah," Dana said. "When Jill began organizing us, what does Otero do? Promote her! And the whole idea fell apart once she left."

"Maybe what Amy did will change things," Adam said, stroking my hair.

"How?" Dana asked, dripping sarcasm.

I picked at a thread on my jeans, wishing we could change the subject.

"Bowing to everyone was an act of respect for others. She was saying all colors are equal."

"So?"

"So when everyone has a chance to think about it, maybe they'll start doing the same thing."

"Don't bet on it," Juan said.

"You know what, Martinez?" Troy's voice turned nasty. "All you've done so far is snipe. How come you let *yourself* be demoted? I'd think you'd want to be a Blue or Dark Green so you could get all that hostility out on us Oranges."

Juan's face flushed and his eyes darted around. In the uncomfortable silence I became aware that he and I were the only minorities in the room. If someone didn't speak up fast, he might just walk out.

"Cut it, Troy," Adam said quickly. "If we're going to fight among ourselves, we won't get anywhere. We have a lot to discuss."

2 **put-down** critical or insulting remark – 16 **to stroke** to pass one's hand lightly over s.th. – 28 **to snipe** to make unpleasant remarks to attack s.o. – 30 **hostility** feeling of hatred or extreme dislike – 31 **to dart** to move about quickly and suddenly – 34 **cut it** stop it

"Right," I piped in, eager to keep our unity and change the subject. "For instance, the papers you No-Teks have to type for us. They're due Friday." I looked up at Adam, holding my breath. "How would you like to type mine, *sweet thing?*" I hadn't planned to ask that way, but it just came out. The last time Adam had asked me to type his paper, he'd called *me* "sweet thing."

Adam's face flushed. "Come on now Amy. You know that's just a joke. Nobody really expects the guys to type the girls' papers."

"Oh, no?" There was a chorus of protest from the girls.

"Of course not. When would I have time? We've got the midterm in Otero's class Friday, and I've got a bio quiz to study for. I've got soccer practice until five Thursday. I've got –"

"Aaah ..." I interrupted, "but you're such a good typist. You got a B-plus in it last year, didn't you, and it shouldn't take long."

"Amy!" Adam's eyes went dark. Maybe he was recalling that these were almost the same words he'd used on me, and the same tone of voice. I almost backed down, but some stubborn instinct kept me gazing up at him with that same kind of puppy-dog helplessness he used on me when he wanted a paper typed. "It's all right, Adam," I said, reaching up to touch his face. "I won't make it too long. And I'll give it to you tomorrow, so you'll have two whole days to get it done." I couldn't believe these words were coming from me.

Adam emitted a resigned groan. "These *Teks,*" he exclaimed with exaggerated sarcasm, "are really something. I'll just have to give it to Dad's secretary."

I opened my mouth to protest, then shut it. I'd gone as far as I dared.

The room rang with the shrill cries of girls and the angry bellows of boys at the injustice of typing the girls' papers. I thought how rare for us to have this kind of power over males, and how uncomfortable. It just didn't feel natural to "use" the boys the way they so often "used" us.

For the rest of the meeting we talked about all kinds of things. The midterm on Friday and what kind of trick questions Otero might ask. Putting out an underground newspaper. The male beauty contest ...

1 **to pipe in** to put in a word – 3 **due** expected to happen or be done at a certain time – 10 **midterm** *(AE)* an examination given in the middle of a term – 11 **quiz** short test – 17 **to back down** to no longer support a certain argument or opinion out of weakness – 23 **to emit** [ɪ'mɪt] to let out – **groan** [grəʊn] *Stöhnen* – 28 **bellow** ['beləʊ] shout with a low deep voice

And planning a rally. That's what stirred the most interest and excitement. If we could somehow show the whole school how we often practice prejudice and injustice without even realizing it ... and do it without G4's finding out and stopping us ... we'd have done something really important. We figured we could hand out petitions, hang up posters, have speakers ... but what we needed was some symbol that would bring us all together as one.

"You know," I mused, "I read that during World War Two the Germans made the Dutch Jews sew stars on their sleeves to set them apart as inferior, so the rest of the Dutch people sewed stars on their sleeves, too. What do you think about us making four-color armbands for everyone to wear, not just the Color Game players?"

Everyone loved the idea, but it meant work, lots of it. We needed materials and sewing machines and plenty of help.

Juan came up with a plan. "My mom does piecework for a dress manufacturer," he said. "We've got boxes and boxes of scrap material at home." A little self-conscious, he added, "If you want, we could all meet at my house next time and work there."

1 **rally** large public political meeting – **to stir** to cause, to produce – 5 **petition** piece of paper demanding or requesting s.th. from those in power – 8 **to muse** ['mju:z] to say in a thoughtful way – 9 **to sew** [səʊ] to fasten with a needle and thread *(nähen)* – **sleeve** part of a shirt, jacket, or coat round the arms – 15 **to do piecework** to work and be paid for the number of products made – 16 **scrap material** material left over when producing s.th. – 17 **self-conscious** nervous, ill at ease

Chapter 10

I was just getting ready to leave for school the next day when the phone rang. Papa had already left and Mama was pulling out of the driveway. She likes to get to Uncle's shop early to help unpack the fresh fish and set it out in the display cases. Uncle says Mama's an artist, that she makes the fish look twice as fresh as it really is, and so beautiful that people enjoy looking as much as buying.

"Hideo?" I asked, immediately sensing something urgent in his voice. "Is anything wrong?"

"It's Sue," he said. "She's not feeling right. Kind of nauseous and crampy. Says it's probably the lobster bisque we ate out last night, but I had it, too, and I didn't bother me. I'm worried. If it weren't for this meeting in San Francisco today, I'd stay home."

"What about her mother?"

"I'd call, but she's a class-A worrier and Sue said she'd never forgive me if I did. I wanted to phone the doctor, but she says I'm making too much of it."

"Do you want me to look in on her after school?"

"Oh, would you, Amy? I'd feel so much better knowing you're with her. When can you get there?"

Wednesdays I tutored Bettina, but I didn't tell Hideo that. I'd just phone and change the date. "I'll be there by three and stay until you get home, so don't worry. She'll be fine. It's probably nothing."

Preoccupied, I went off to school hoping Sue wasn't going to lose the baby. A slight drizzle turned into a steady rain and I ran the last block holding my zippered notebook over my head.

Just as I reached the school steps Brian stopped me. He seemed to be waiting just for me, or was I being paranoid?

"Hello, Amy," he greeted. "Typical of an Orange – being late. Let's see your journal."

"Now?"

"Now. Your journal, please."

2 **to pull out** to drive away from – 9 **nauseous** [ˈnɔːʃəs] feeling sick *(übel)* – 10 **crampy** with severe pains from the tightening of muscles – **lobster** *Hummer* – **bisque** [bɪsk] *(French)* a thick cream soup with fish – **to eat out** to eat in a restaurant – 14 **class-A** *(ironic) here:* terrible; *usu.* of the best quality – 23 **preoccupied** paying no attention to the outside world because of worrying – 24 **drizzle** light rain – 25 **zippered** *(AE)* closed with a zipper *(Reißverschluss)* – 27 **paranoid** believing that everyone wants to harm and mistreat you

"Can I just get out of the rain?"

"You'll stand here until I see that journal!"

Why was he doing this? Because I wouldn't go out with him? Other students rushed by, barely noticing, intent on getting under cover. There was nothing to do except give him the journal as fast as possible so I could be done with it and get into school. I shivered as the rain wet through my sweater, but unzipped my notebook, pulled out the journal, and handed it to him.

Waiting there, notebook on head, getting wetter by the minute from the slanting rain, I hated him and hated the way he made me feel, stupid, and unimportant, and ... without value. I tried to stand proudly as if I didn't care, thinking that if he'd offered to share his umbrella at that moment, I'd refuse. At last, after what seemed minutes, during which he browsed slowly through the pages of my journal, he returned it to me and waved me on.

"Thanks, Brian," I said coldly. "You're a real sport."

"Thought you needed a lesson, Amy. Your fellow Blues are really pissed off about you. They're out to get you for betraying them, so watch it!"

Betraying them? I troubled over Brian's words all the way to my first class, where I arrived cold, wet, and late. When I fell into my seat, someone poked me in the shoulder. "Oranges sit in back," Carol said, a gleam of satisfaction in her eyes, "behind their superiors."

"Oh, for goodness sakes!" I exclaimed. "That's ridiculous."

"I'm just going by the rules," she added. "The way *you* should have!"

"Carol? Amy?" the teacher called out so the whole class turned to look at us.

Seething, but not wanting to make a scene, I picked up my books, turned my back on Carol, and took another seat. Being an Orange seemed such a hassle, having to bow so much, be on guard all the time, take insults from everyone and pretend it didn't hurt. I felt so unbalanced by it all that I couldn't settle down to concentrate.

We'd been assigned to read *Down These Mean Streets,* a book by

4 **intent on doing s.th.** eager to do s.th. – 6 **to shiver** to shake slightly – 10 **to slanting** not coming straight down, but from the side – 14 **to browse** [braʊz] to look through in a casual way – 18 **pissed off** *(slang)* irritated – **to be out to get s.o.** to want to harm s.o. – 23 **gleam** a pale light; an expression on s.o.'s face – 24 **for goodness sake** an expression of annoyance – 29 **to seethe** to be extremely angry – 31 **hassle** ['hæsl] struggle, difficulty – 33 **to settle down** to begin to turn one's attention to s.th.

Piri Thomas about being Puerto Rican. So that's what we talked about in Otero's class that day. The book was about Thomas's life in the streets, stealing and dealing drugs. He "looked" black and when his family moved to a mostly white neighborhood, he didn't fit in. Just like when you change colors in the Color Game, I thought, glancing down at my blue and orange color bands.

Pretty soon the Latinos and other minorities in class got to talking, telling the kinds of things you only tell really good friends. They almost seemed to forget where they were or who was listening.

"My grandfather crossed the border when he was only twelve," Raúl said. "He came from such poor people, they couldn't afford to feed him. He worked as a farm laborer most of his life, fourteen hours a day, and sent money 'home.' "

"My father was a Vietnam hero," Gwen said. "But when he got out of the service, he couldn't get a job. Because he was *black.*"

"It's not just color that makes it so hard," Juan added, "it's being poor. When you have very little money you can't afford decent housing so you live where it's crowded and noisy, where crime and drugs are a way of life because it's the only way to get money. Your kids don't eat well, so they're sick more often, and doctors cost. Poverty is what separates people, maybe even more than color."

"It's a vicious circle, a Catch-22," Otero said. "If *color* prevents you from getting work, because you're labeled inferior, you lose your self-respect and ambition. You can't support a family and, feeling guilty, may leave them. The family suffers. The children see how their parents couldn't make it because of color, so maybe they don't even try. But things are changing. They appear to be getting better. Education is still the ladder to economic success."

I don't think we arrived at any real conclusions, but when the bell rang I felt a closeness among the students that hadn't been there before. I guess it was from opening up to each other. Maybe it wouldn't last, but at least it was a beginning.

I phoned Mrs. Tarcher right after class, a lump of fear settling in my stomach. Adam waited nearby, talking with friends. Somehow his mother always made me feel awkward without reason, guilty without cause. "Mrs. Tarcher?" I asked in a voice not at all mine.

11 **Raúl** [ra'ul] – 22 **vicious** ['vɪʃəs] **circle** *Teufelskreis* – **Catch-22** from the 1961 war novel *Catch-22* by Joseph Heller. *Catch-22* refers to a rule that is so paradoxical that there is no way to properly follow it. – 23 **to label** to describe or classify s.th. or s.o. – 33 **lump** heavy compact mass – **to settle** to come to rest – 35 **awkward** ['ɔːkwəd] uncomfortable, uneasy

"Yes?"

"This is Amy. Amy Sumoto."

"Yes? What is it, Amy?"

I told her about Sue and how I'd make up Bettina's lesson Saturday if it would be convenient.

"This is very short notice," Adam's mother said. "If I'd known before Bettina left for school, I'd have made other arrangements."

"I didn't want to phone too early," I explained, "for fear of waking you. I'm sorry."

"I'm not sure about Saturday," she said, ignoring my apology. "I'll let you know."

"All right. Good-bye ..." I hung up. She hadn't offered a word of sympathy about Sue – not a word. How could Adam be so kind and warm and his mother so cold and unfeeling?

Getting to the phone had taken some doing. In just one day of being an Orange, I'd discovered the secret to survival – anonymity. If you walked briskly or smiled or made eye contact you were sure to be stopped by a G4 or a higher color. So, I did the opposite. Whenever I saw a G4 headed my way, I about-faced, or hid in a cluster of regular students, eyes averted. It never occurred to me, until I did that, how many kids just blended into the background routinely in school.

Adam drove me to Sue's place right after school. "We need to talk," I said. "But not now." We kissed quickly, then he drove off, already late for soccer practice.

Hideo had said he'd leave a key under a flowerpot so I wouldn't have to disturb Sue. I found the key and opened the door, calling out Sue's name so as not to scare her.

"In here," she answered from the bedroom.

She was in bed, hair tousled like a sleepy child's and face unusually pale. She gave me a wan smile.

I dropped my books on the floor and bent to kiss her. "Hi, how's it going? Want some tea?"

"No ... no ... nothing. Just sit down and keep me company."

4 **to make up** to do s.th. later that couldn't be done earlier – 5 **convenient** suitable, not causing any problems – 6 **short notice** without enough warning – 16 **anonymity** [ˌænəˈnɪmətɪ] not being an individual person – 17 **briskly** quickly – 19 **to about-face** *(AE)* to turn so as to be in the opposite direction – 20 **to avert** to turn away – 21 **to blend into s.th.** to combine with s.th. so as to no longer be noticeably different – 29 **tousled** [ˈtaʊzld] disarranged, untidy – 30 **wan** [wɒn] appearing weak and tired – 33 **to keep s.o. company** to stay with s.o. so that the person has s.o. to talk to

I sat on the bed facing her and took her hand. "Are you okay? Are the cramps gone?"

She shook her head. "No. But let's not talk about that. Just talk to me."

I told her about things at school, and about the plans we'd made for the rally. I told her about Adam, how we seemed to be edgy with each other, how I found myself holding back since I'd found out about his weekend party.

She watched me, eyes glistening, but I felt she was someplace else, listening to some inner sounds, rather than to me. She seemed to need my presence and the monotone of my voice, so I talked on. I had about run out of things to say when Sue drew her hand away, turned her head and began to cry. My heart lurched.

"Sue, Sue! What is it?"

"Oh, Amy, I'm so scared!" She sobbed.

I waited for her to go on, afraid of what she'd say, but after a time she turned back to me, eyes wet and red. "I've been hemorrhaging."

"Oh, no."

"We want this baby so much. It means so much to us, to ... everything ..."

"I know, I know," I crooned. "Listen, I'll call the doctor."

She shook her head. "I phoned already. The only thing I can do is stay in bed and rest. He wants to see me tomorrow."

"Maybe it will be all right. Sometimes it happens ..." What did I know about pregnancy? Yet it seemed the only hopeful thing to say. "Should I call Hideo?"

"He's in San Francisco."

I jumped up. "I'll phone Mama. Papa." My mind raced. Mama might be at the store, or on her way home. Papa might be anywhere. Sue's mother lived out of town, too far away to come quickly. Before I'd even left the room, Sue stopped me.

"Amy, no. Please ..."

"Why, Sue? Why not?"

She started to cry then, really cry. Big, deep sobs with her hands

6 **edgy** nervous, easily irritated – 9 **to glisten** ['glɪsn] to shine because of tears – 13 **to lurch** to move with strong and sudden, irregular movements – 15 **to sob** *schluchzen* – 17 **to hemorrhage** ['hemərɪdʒ] to lose a lot of blood – 21 **to croon** [kruːn] to say in a soft pleasant voice – 25 **pregnancy** condition of having an unborn child in the body

over her eyes. I came back to the bed and put my arms around her, rocking her to me, back and forth.

"Everything depends on this baby," she mumbled into my shoulder. "Everything. It's not just that *we* want it. It's so important to your parents. It's the only way they'll really accept me. I can't stand to see how it tears Hideo apart – this ... strangeness ... since we married. He needs them, your parents. Their acceptance and love. The baby ... makes all the difference."

"Oh, no, Sue. No. That's not true. Really! My parents love you. They just don't know how to show it. Give them time. They don't show emotion much, but how could they *not* love you?"

And I thought, oh, Mama, Papa. How could you hurt this sweet, good woman – just because she's not Japanese?

Mama and Papa arrived shortly before Hideo reached home. They came into the bedroom carrying flowers from our garden. For Sue's sake, I wished Mama would kiss her, or Papa would touch her arm – some gesture of love. But it was not their way. Mama almost immediately bustled into the kitchen to put the flowers in water and fix a special tea she said would help stop the bleeding. And Papa sat on a kitchen chair, hands in lap, looking awkward and miserable.

"I'm so sorry," Sue apologized, trying hard for cheerfulness. "I really should get up and fix something ... Mama shouldn't have to –"

Papa waved her back. "No ... daughter-in-law ..." Immediately he corrected himself. "No, Sue. You must do what the doctor says. Rest flat in bed. We do not want anything to happen to your baby, our grandchild. Or to you."

16 **for s.o.'s sake** in order to help s.o. – 18 **to bustle** ['bʌsl] **into s.th.** to move busily and energetically into s.th. – 20 **lap** the upper part of the legs when seated

Chapter 11

Journal entry, Friday, November 3: I can't believe Otero's test.

The G4's handed out the question sheets as soon as the bell rang. *By color.* Which meant we Oranges got the questions last.

Full of impossible multiple choice and true-false, and even essay questions, it was so hard and long I didn't even finish. But others did. When I looked up, about thirty-five minutes into the test, Blues and Dark Greens were leaving in droves. They seemed to find it easy.

"How come?" I asked when we gathered outside the classroom afterward. "Could they be smarter?"

Juan snorted.

"It had to be rigged," Adam said. "Otero's trying to teach us one of his little 'lessons.' Probably trying to say that poor people and ethnic groups don't test well because of language problems and cultural differences."

Of course he was right. Success in school does depend a whole lot on test taking. Which doesn't make me feel better, considering I expect to fail.

Sue lost the baby.

I learned of it when I reached home. She answered the phone in such a dead tone that I knew right away. "No, please don't come now," she said. "Hideo is here and I just want to be quiet. Tonight, if you like. I'm going back to work Monday. It will be good seeing the ..." Her voice trailed off as if she couldn't bring herself to say "children."

I hung up and sat for a long time just staring out the window at Mama's garden. My throat felt tight with tears. It took a long time to find positive things to think – that Sue was young and could have other children. Small consolations.

When Mama and Papa reached home I told them the news. Mama nodded, and went immediately to fix supper. "It will be hard for them," she said quietly. "No matter how many children they have, they'll always wonder about this one, the one they lost."

Papa went to the sink to wash his hands as usual, then sat down at the table and picked up the newspaper.

7 **in droves** in large groups – 10 **to snort** *verächtlich schnauben* – 23 **to trail off** to become slowly silent – 28 **consolation** s.th. that gives comfort in a time of sadness

"We should go over there tonight," I said, watching Papa and growing angrier with each second of his silence.

"Yes," Mama said.

"You're not fair to Sue, Papa!" I burst on. It was so uncharacteristic for me to raise my voice that Papa looked up and his eyes grew big and dark. Before he could stop me I raced on. "Hideo loves her! Can't you see it in his eyes? Don't you care that she makes him happy?" I wiped tears from my cheeks. "She needs to know that you accept her, that you like her and maybe someday may even love her! Can't you open your heart a *little,* Papa? Can't you?"

"That's enough, Emiko," Papa cried. "Quite enough! The egg doesn't tell the chicken how to act!"

"Papa!" I cried, then closed my mouth and lowered my eyes at the warning look on his face. Mama turned away, busying herself at the stove.

It was hard to love Papa at this moment. Though I'd grown up without many words of love, without much touching, at least from my father, I always knew that deep down, he cared. But now that wasn't enough. He needed to *show* something of his feelings. Sue came from a family in which words and gestures of love were part of every day. She thrived on it, and she gave it generously; maybe that's why she made Hideo so happy.

Unable to let it go, I asked, "What can we do for her, Mama, what?"

Papa shook his head in annoyance, put down the newspaper, and strode from the room. I supposed he would run off to his workshop, his hideaway from the world.

Mama wiped her hands and came to the table. She touched my arm. "Come with me, Emiko, I want to show you something."

I followed Mama up the stairs to her workroom. It's where she sews and does bills, and writes letters to our big family in Hawaii and Utah. Once she showed me some haiku she had written, hand trembling as she offered the pages to me. "I don't know if they are any good," she said.

They were beautiful poems, whole scenes compacted into a few words, full of feeling, perfect miniatures. She had flushed with pleasure at my delight.

21 **to thrive on s.th.** to develop or grow well because of s.th. – 24 **annoyance** irritation – 30 **to do bills** *(AE)* to write checks to pay bills *(Rechnungen)* – 31 **haiku** ['haɪku:] a short Japanese poem usually on the subject of nature

Mama went right to the carved black-and-gold chest that had come over from Japan with Grandpa, and opened it. She lifted several things out of the way, then removed two packages wrapped in brightly colored tissue paper.

"This, I made for the baby ... and this ..."

I brought the packages to the small couch and sat down to open them. In the first I found a mobile. Origami birds in brilliant colors suspended by string from a smooth wooden rod, something Papa must have made in his workshop. My throat tightened. They were so like the mobile Mama had made years ago to hang over my bed. I seemed to recall the sunny bedroom of my infancy and the many hours when I watched with wonder or reached for these colorful birds who flew above me with each breath of wind.

Mama watched anxiously as I opened the second package. It contained a tiny pale-green sweater, cap, and booties. Tears came to my eyes and then Mama said, "Come with me."

Wondering what more she had to show, I followed her into her bedroom. There, on the black lacquered table near the window, stood the bonsai in its earthenware pot that has been in our family for two hundred years. Bonsai is an art form passed down from father to son. The plants are pruned and fertilized so that they grow into dwarf versions of ancient stately trees. Our family's bonsai was special in that it consisted of not one tree, but a grouping which suggested a wooded mountainside.

I looked to Mama, questioningly.

"Papa planned to give this to Hideo when the child was born. I think, now, he will give it to him anyway."

Mama's eyes held mine, and I understood more in that look than words could say. I went to her and put my arms around her and we stood that way together for many moments.

1 **carved** *geschnitzt* – **chest** *Truhe* – 4 **tissue** ['tɪʃu:] **paper** light thin paper – 7 **mobile** ['məʊˌbi:l] a work of art with objects hanging from a wire or string – 8 **rod** long thin pole – 11**infancy** ['ɪnfənsɪ] early childhood – 15 **pale-green** light, not bright green – 18 **lacquered** ['lækəd] *lackiert* – 19 **bonsai** ['bɒnsaɪ] – **earthenware** made of rough baked clay *(Ton)* – 21 **to prune** to cut the branches of a tree or bush shorter so that it has a better form – **to fertilize** *düngen* – **dwarf** much smaller than the usual size – 22 **stately** impressive in style or size

Hideo answered the door to us that evening. He looked so drawn, so strained, as if he could hardly keep control. Without a word I embraced him, and then Mama did. Papa, behind us, carried the bonsai.

Hideo greeted Papa, then his eyes fell to the plant. He took a deep breath and his glance returned to Papa. Then he rubbed an eye and said, "Come in. Sue's in bed. I was just making tea."

Mama started taking off her coat. "I brought some cakes. I'll fix the tea. You all go in to Sue."

Hideo brought me and Papa into the bedroom. "We've been having an argument. Sue thinks she can go back to school Monday as if nothing has happened. I say she should stay home a few days at least. That's what the doctor says, too."

"I can't – don't you understand? I feel so useless, so empty ..." Sue sounded all choked up. "I'll be all right. Just let me get back to work."

"You will not go to work!"

"That's my decision, Hideo, not yours!"

Papa had quietly placed the bonsai on the dresser, but Sue had been so intensely involved with Hideo that she had not even noticed. Now Papa stood at the head of the bed. "Hideo is right. You must take care of yourself. For your own sake, as well as his. And for all of us ... who care."

Sue opened her mouth to speak, then her eyes closed and tears slowly slid down her cheeks. Hideo took her into his arms. When she finally gained control, Hideo said, "Look, honey, what Papa has brought us."

Sue wiped her eyes and blew her nose as Hideo brought the bonsai to the bedside table. "It's ... beautiful," she cried in awe. "So beautiful!" Eyes sparkling with tears, she looked at Papa.

"It is a small piece of Japan to remind you and Hideo of our heritage," he said. "When your son is born, Sue – and you *will* have a son one day – he must learn from Hideo how to care for it so that he, too, can pass it on."

1 **drawn** tired and worried – 2 **strained** very tired and anxious – **to embrace** to take s.o. in one's arms as a sign of liking or loving s.o. – 4 **choked up** unable to speak or breathe properly because of great emotion – 17 **dresser** *(AE)* chest of drawers *(BE)* *(Kommode)* – 27 **in awe** [ɔː] with a feeling of respect mixed with fear or wonder – 29 **heritage** ['herɪtɪdʒ] customs and traditions that have been passed down from generation to generation

“Oh!” Sue exclaimed. “Oh, my! I’m going to cry again! Thank you. Thank you so much, Papa Sumoto,” she whispered.

Mama bustled in, smiling, carrying a tray with teapot and cups and a platter of luscious-looking sweets. She poured the tea and soon we were talking and laughing like a real family. And as we left, Sue’s eyes were shining again as she looked from the bonsai to Hideo, and to Papa.

When I lay in bed later, thinking about this evening, I felt different, somehow. It was good to be who I was, part of a rich culture ... good to be Japanese.

4 **platter** large dish for serving food – **luscious** [ˈlʌʃəs] delicious

Chapter 12

I tutored Tina Saturday morning, then went straight home. Adam was picking me up to go to Juan's house. Juan had spoken to some of his Light Green pals and they'd be there, too. With so many working, we hoped to get all the posters and four-color armbands finished for the rally Wednesday.

"This game of Otero's is a pain in the you-know-what," Adam said, settling down next to me in the car. "I've got to carry my journal around even on the soccer field! And I'll be darned if I'll have anything to do with that beauty contest."

"Poor baby," I teased.

Adam messed my hair in response. "I mean it. I'll play hooky before I'll go prancing around like Arnold Schwarzenegger in my gym shorts!"

"What if it had been a *female* beauty contest?"

"That's different."

"Why?"

"Because women are pretty, which men aren't." He leered at me and backed off as I pretended to punch him.

"Adam Tarcher, you're a real male chauvinist –"

"– hunk."

"You'll be the best-looking man there, you know. The girls will be all over you."

Adam gave a long-suffering sigh, quite obviously pleased at the prospect. "That's what I'm afraid off." He started the car and put an arm around me. Now would be a good time to ask about the mountain weekend. So far he hadn't said a word to me and I hadn't asked. I wondered how to phrase the question without sounding suspicious or jealous.

"By the way," I said, trying for lightness, "how was the party?"

3 **pal** *(informal)* good friend – 6 **pain in the you-know-what** polite way of saying "pain in the ass", i.e. s.th. or s.o. that is very irritating – 8 **darned** polite way of saying "damned" – 11 **to play hooky** ['hʊkɪ] *(AE)* to stay away from school without permission – 12 **to prance around** to move about arrogantly with a dancing step – **Arnold Schwarzenegger** Austrian-born body-builder and Hollywood actor – 17 **to leer at s.o.** to smile unpleasantly at s.o. with sexual desire – 19 **male chauvinist** ['ʃəʊvɪnɪst] man who thinks all men are better than women, macho – 24 **prospect** possibility that s.th. might happen – 28 **jealous** *eifersüchtig*

He glanced at me, puzzled, then looked back at the road. "Party? What party?"

"Tina said you invited a bunch of good friends ... you know, Beth and Eileen ... some others ... to your mountain house." I bit my lip to hold back the rest of what I wanted to ask, like how come he hadn't included me. Didn't he think I was good enough for him?

Adam frowned ... seemed to be struggling to understand, then he slapped the steering wheel. "Tina! That brat! I should have known!"

I waited for him to go on.

He looked away from the road. "What did she tell you?"

My throat tightened with the same ache I'd felt when Tina first told me. "She said you'd invited all these ... very good friends to sleep over." I gave a light laugh. "But I figured that since *I* wasn't invited ..."

Adam swerved suddenly and pulled over to the curb. He shut off the motor and turned to me. "Amy, how could you? How could you believe that little troublemaker sister of mine? You know me better than that!"

I lowered my eyes and bit my lip.

"I didn't invite those kids beforehand! It was no planned thing. The guys who came over are from families who have winter places just like ours. They come up every year, the same weekend, just like us. We get together ... traditionally. It means nothing!" He took my hands in his. "You surely didn't think ..."

When I didn't immediately answer he asked, "You do believe me, don't you?"

"I suppose." But a small doubt did persist. What he'd said about Juan in that moment of anger couldn't be ignored. His mother's attitude. My own father's. Could he, could I, escape their prejudices? I bent my head, staring at Adam's strong hands, which were gripping my own smaller ones so firmly.

"Amy. Look at me."

When I raised my eyes his face was very serious and troubled. "I thought I didn't need Otero's game to show me that our differences weren't important. Now I know better. I liked you from the beginning ... because of the kind of person you are."

I stiffened, not knowing just what he meant. "You bring me something new from what I've always known, in little ways – the way you do things, the way you think, your femininity, your courage, your

14 **to swerve** to turn suddenly to one side – 26 **to persist** to continue – 29 **to grip** to hold tightly

sensitivity, your creativity ... You *are* different ... but that's what I love."

"Hold me, Adam ... please ..."

Without another word he brought me into his arms and held me close, pressing his lips against my hair. And then he kissed me, as softly and lovingly as if I were terribly fragile and precious. It felt right and good and the doubts fled to a distant place. We kissed again, this time laughing and with little joyful yelps, so very glad it was right between us once more. And then Adam remembered we were due at Juan's. I curled close to him, nestling my head against his shoulder, and in a moment we were on the road again.

Juan lived in a mostly Latino neighborhood, poorer than where I lived. The homes were closer together and not as well kept. Young children cluttered the cracked sidewalks on tricycles or skates.

Adam parked the BMW between a beat-up VW and a vintage 1960 Ford and we climbed the creaky steps to a landing. Laughter and voices came from within. Through lace-curtained windows we glimpsed a dozen or more kids from our class milling about.

Juan answered the door, face flushed with excitement. "Come in, come in! We started already. You should see what we've done! We've got two sewing machines going and some guys have been here since morning!" He drew us inside and gestured triumphantly.

The L-shaped living-dining room vibrated with sound. A TV was blaring. A radio was playing salsa music somewhere in the back of the house. A baby cried and a loud voice called out in Spanish.

On the wall opposite the door above a worn couch my eye immediately caught sight of a portrait of John F. Kennedy on a black velvet background.

8 **yelp** short high cry of joy – 9 **to be due** to be expected to arrive – 10 **to nestle** ['nesl] to move into a comfortable position – 14 **to clutter** to move about in a disrodeerly manner – **cracked** broken, damaged – **tricyle** a vehicle similar to a bicycle, but with three wheels instead of two – **skates** roller-skates – 15 **beat-up** in poor condition – **vintage** old enough to be in a museum – 16 **creaky** ['kri:kɪ] noisy when stepped on – **landing** floor area in between sets of stairs – 17 **lace** kind of material with a pattern of openings *(Spitze)* – 18 **to mill about** to move about without any purpose – 24 **to blare** to produce loud and unpleasant sounds – **salsa** ['sɔ:lsə] **music** a kind of Puerto-Rican big-band dance music – 26 **worn** showing signs of a lot of use or wear – 27 **John F. Kennedy** (1925–1963) President of the U.S.A. from 1961–1963. At the time he was killed he was on the point of suggesting laws to protect the rights of minorities. – **velvet** soft cloth with a thick layer of short, cut threads on one side *(Samt)*

"Hey, guys, quiet down!" Troy shouted from the dining area. "I can't hear myself think!"

Juan stepped over some boxes and turned the TV low. Fellow students greeted us from all over the room. Some were sorting through boxes overflowing with colorful materials, or ripping long strips of fabric into narrow strands. Some sat on the floor sewing strips together, or just fooling around.

Juan led us to a large box and pulled out a ring of new four-color bands. "We've already got about two hundred of these. By tonight we should have enough for the whole school!"

"You're so well organized," Adam said, putting an arm around my shoulders, "that you don't even need us. C'mon, honey. Let's go."

"Not so fast!" Juan grabbed us. "Amy's assigned poster duty. You can help, too, Adam. She's good at lettering. *You* can paint in the colors."

And so we joined the work force of some twenty or more classmates. Despite the noise and a kind of mad chaos, it was fun lettering the ALL COLORS UNITE signs. I felt part of something important, not like when I'd been a Blue and no one wanted to do anything together, because they already had what they wanted.

At one point, half listening to the talk around me, I thought that it must have been like this in pioneer days – when women gathered to make quilts on long winter evenings. Keeping hands busy, they'd talk of children and crops and their hopes for the future. Our talk wasn't all that different – about teachers and movies and friends. And about the Color Game.

Michelle told how a G4 accused her of *stealing*. "Can you imagine? Why would I try to steal some stupid play money? I bet they'd never have dared accuse me if I were a Dark Green or Blue!"

Kevin told how he hated being promoted Light Green so late in the game. "It's hard, shifting loyalties. In my heart I'm still an Orange, and the Light Greens treat me like an outsider! I'm caught in no-man's-land, in limbo."

About four o'clock Juan's mother, a pretty woman with a bashful smile, came in from the kitchen. She carried a big tray with a pitcher

5 **to rip** to tear quickly or violently – 6 **fabric** ['fæbrɪk] cloth, material – 13 **to assign s.th. to s.o.** to give s.o. a specific task – **poster duty** the job of preparing the posters – 23 **quilt** blanket made up of small patches of material sewn together – 33 **in limbo** in a place between two worlds – 34 **bashful** shy and self-conscious – 35 **pitcher** large container for liquids

of Kool-Aid and a platter of nachos and quesadillas, cheese-filled tortillas. The sweet smell of corn and melted cheese filled the room. I couldn't help thinking how Juan's family may not have had money but their riches were in closeness to each other.

"Ah, food," Adam said, looking up from the poster he was painting. "I'm starved. Get me a plate of those, will you, honey?" He flashed me one of his winning smiles.

Without thinking I stopped work on the intricate lettering and got up. Then I realized what was happening. My face got hot and my heart began to race as I sat down again.

"Adam, honey," I said sweetly, picking up my pen again. "I'm starved, too. Would *you* mind getting the drinks and nachos?"

Troy, working with us, looked up in surprise. Maybe he heard something different in my voice, because Adam stared at me, too, startled. My legs began to shake and my lips to tremble, but I didn't back down.

Half the kids were clustered around the food by now, but Adam still didn't move. Finally, he put his paintbrush down and stood up. A small, secret smile crossed his lips. And without a word he went off to get our snacks.

By six o'clock the room looked like a disaster area. Scraps of material lay everywhere. Finished posters and banners were stacked on top of every surface, and boxes overflowed with the bands we'd made. Before leaving we went over the plans for Wednesday one more time. Troy would have the protest flyers photocopied and ready to hand out. We'd all be at school early to help put up the signs and banners. Teams of two would pass out the new color bands all around the school.

"This has been great," Adam said as we joined the others leaving. "The G4's are gonna have a cow when they see the whole school behind us."

"The Blues and Dark Greens will have to join us or they'll become the outcasts," Juan added.

Everyone was thanking Juan and his mother and carrying out the posters and boxes, but we were leaving a terrible mess. I started

1 **Kool-Aid** *(trademark)* sweet drink with artificial fruit flavor – **nachos** [ˈnɒːtʃəʊz] Mexican dish made up of corn chips eaten with melted cheese – **quesadilla** [ˌkeɪsəˈdiːjə] tortilla folded over cheese and onions and fried – **tortilla** [tɔːˈtiːjə] thin round piece of dough made of cornmeal *(=Maismehl)* – 8 **intricate** [ˈɪntrɪkət] complex, complicated – 22 **to be stacked** to be in a pile or heap – 25 **flyer** leaflet – 30 **to have a cow** *(slang)* to be very surprised

picking up some of the bigger scraps, but Juan waved me away. "No, scram. I'll do it." His mother nodded agreement.

I felt an enormous rush of affection for them both. Juan's mother worked full-time, but she'd spent her whole day off helping us whenever the sewing machines jammed or anyone needed something. The hospitality and warmth had somehow changed all of us. We had come separately, but were leaving as a family.

We stood talking and laughing out on the street while posters and boxes were put in different cars, when my eye caught something odd. A bright red Toyota station wagon pulled up to the curb across the street and someone familiar stepped out. Brian! Brian and Mary! What were they doing here? A surge of fear rushed down my arms and I stepped in front of Adam to hide what he was doing from view. "Adam ... Adam, look!" I whispered. He straightened up from loading a box of armbands into the trunk. Leaning against the fender in plain sight were half a dozen brightly painted posters.

"Oh, no! No! Where did they come from?" Adam slammed the trunk lid shut and stepped back. Others had seen the G4's and hurried over to our car. Juan must have noticed from inside the house, because suddenly he flew down the stairs and joined us.

"What are you doing here, Brian? Mary?" Adam challenged. "What do you want?"

"What are *you* doing here?" Brian crossed his arms over his chest while Mary went around the car, spying.

"This was a private party ... of Oranges," Juan said, although standing right next to him was a Light Green. "We have a right to meet, so what do you want?"

Mary, of course, found the posters and held one up for Brian to see. She pulled a handful of new wristbands from a box and dangled them from her fingers like dirty laundry.

"Just a private party, huh?" Brian asked.

"There's nothing illegal about what we were doing," I said, trying to keep the tremor from my voice. "We have a right to organize. We had to organize!"

2 **scram** leave quickly – 5 **to jam** to no longer function because s.th. has got stuck – 10 **station wagon** *(AE) Kombi* – 12 **surge** rush, sudden feeling – 15 **fender** *(AE)* mudguard *(BE)* the part of a car above or over the wheels – 16 **in plain sight** so easily seen that it can't be overlooked – 21 **to challenge** to question the rightness or legality of s.th. – 29 **wrist** [rɪst] the joint that joins the hand to the arm – **to dangle** to hang loosely – 30 **laundry** ['lɔːndrɪ] clothes or sheets that need to be washed – 33 **tremor** ['tremə] nervous shaking

"So you're the ringleader, Amy? I'm surprised at you!"

Adam put an arm around me. "We're all responsible, and I don't see what you can do about it!"

"Oh, that's easy. We confiscate this stuff and that's that. No rally Wednesday."

"How do you know it's Wednesday?"

Brian smiled. "We have our ways."

"You can't do that!"

"Oh, yes we can!"

"Wait a minute!" I called out. "Who told you? This was a secret meeting!"

Brian shrugged, while Mary started stacking armloads of posters near the red car. "We know everything you Oranges are up to. That's how we keep our power."

"Yeah! How *did* you know? Who told on us?" Troy called out from the small crowd that had gathered. "It had to be one of us!" He looked first at me, then at Juan.

"Aw, cut it, Troy. Quit that," Adam said. "You're doing just what Brian wants, making us all suspicious of each other."

"Yeah? Well, you tell me. One of us ratted. Those guys aren't clairvoyant! How about it, Brian?"

Brian smiled enigmatically, leaning against our car, arms wrapped around himself. He made me so angry, my legs began shaking. "Okay, everyone," he said. "Get to work. Move that stuff to my car."

I stepped forward. "No! No way!"

Brian laughed, ignoring me. "Mary, get those guys to open their car trunks. They probably have them loaded with rally stuff."

"No!" I cried in such a sharp voice that a few of the Oranges who had started back to their cars stopped. "We're not helping you. And we're not letting you take our stuff."

"She's right! Yeah!"

"Listen, Amy. You're just a lowly Orange. Be a smart Tek and do what you're told." He tried to put a comradely arm around my shoulder, but I shook him off.

1 **ringleader** person who leads others in doing s.th. wrong – 4 **to confiscate** to take s.th. away from s.o. as a punishment – 15 **to tell on s.o.** to let people in authority know about other people's secret activities – 20 **to rat** *(AE)* to betray, to tell on s.o. – **clairvoyant** [kleə'vɔɪənt] able to know what is in the minds of others – 22 **enigmatically** [ˌenɪg'mætɪklɪ] mysteriously

"Don't be so condescending. We worked hard on the rally stuff. What you're trying to do is ... oppression. We won't stand for it. We have the right to put on a rally."

"Well, well, just listen to the girl," Brian mocked, but his manner became less assured. "Little Amy speaks out for the masses!"

"She's right," Adam called, turning around to the others. Let's put those posters back in our cars; they're ours."

Brian's smile disappeared. Mary rushed to his side. "I'm warning you, Adam ..."

"What more can you do than you've already done?" Adam asked. He opened the car trunk and we started loading posters again.

"Otero will ... the other G4's ..." Brian threw out threats as fast as gunfire while we went on loading, pretending to ignore him. Everyone else in our group went back to their cars, too, working even faster than before.

"You'll hear from us!" Brian threatened as I climbed into the car beside Adam. "There'll be no rally Wednesday. Just remember that!" he shouted.

Adam pulled away from the curb and waited until the three other cars pulled out behind us. Brian remained in the middle of the road, hands on his hips, still shouting threats. Mary behind him, grinned and gave us the victory sign.

"We did it!" Adam said, softly. "We really did it!"

"We did, we did!" I cried. "And nothing's going to stop that rally Wednesday!"

"You're a tiger," Adam said, shaking his head in admiration. "A real tiger. Wow!"

I giggled. And then I slid next to him, laid my head against his shoulder, and growled a proper tiger growl.

1 **condescending** behaving in a way that shows that one thinks one is better than others – 12 **threat** [θret] a warning that you will hurt or harm s.o. if that person does not do what you want

Chapter 13

"What you got in there, girl?" Paul asked on Monday, peering over my shoulder in the hallway. "Gonna dynamite the school or something?" He laughed, as if he knew more than he was saying.

"Nothing. Just some old gym clothes."

He'd caught me stuffing my backpack, loaded with the new armbands, into my locker. I tried to look innocent, but my face burned hot as I slammed the locker door and twirled the combination.

"Gym clothes, hunh? I'll just bet."

I thought, *He knows all about the Saturday meeting at Juan's and our fight with the G4's! Either I'm paranoid or he also knows exactly what I was hiding for Wednesday's rally.*

"Ready for the beauty contest?" I asked, changing the subject.

"Oranges don't talk to Blues unless spoken to. See you in class, Amy. Be good." He sauntered down the hall, turning once to smile knowingly at me.

It seemed that most of the school had heard about our run-in with Brian and Mary. You could sense a difference. I read a kind of grudging admiration in the way some people smiled or said hello. Even the G4's and the higher colors acted differently. During the whole morning not one of them stopped me to bow or show my journal. When we passed, they looked away or through me, as if I didn't exist. Being ignored wasn't any pleasanter than being challenged for every little thing.

Just before Otero's class I met Gwen in the rest room. She hadn't spoken a word to mc sincc I was demoted, so I washed my hands and combed my hair and studiously avoided looking at her after the expccted bow.

"Only four more days and the game's over," she said, watching me in the mirror.

"I know. It's been interesting."

"It's all right. You can talk. I won't report you."

"What do you want to talk about?" I turned around to face her. "Did you hear what happened Saturday?"

7 **to twirl** to cause to turn around quickly – **combination** combination lock, a lock that can only be opened when a moveable part is turned to certain numbers – 8 **hunh?** [hən] an exclamation used when asking a question – **I'll just bet!** I don't believe you! – 14 **to saunter** ['sɔ:ntə] to walk without being in a hurry – 16 **run-in** quarrel, disagreement – 17 **grudging** very unwilling – 26 **studiously** ['stju:dɪəslɪ] carefully

"I did. But be careful. Something's going on. Otero's been huddling with the G4's. They're going to stop that rally, somehow."

"Would you tell me, if you knew how?"

Gwen hesitated, looked away for a moment, then said, "Maybe."

"Why?"

"You're suspicious because I'm a Blue? Because I told you I like being top dog?"

I shrugged.

"I didn't say I would," she said, "only maybe. I never thought those white dudes you hang around with would get anything from this game. But it looks like they're beginning to understand how it is for us a lot of the time. So ... *maybe.*"

"Well, if you do hear anything ..."

"Yeah. I'll think about it."

"Well, on to Otero's class," I said. Being nearest the exit door, I should have left first. But Gwen was a Blue. For an awkward second all that the Color Game stood for passed between us. Then I made a sweeping gesture to indicate she had the right of way, and she shook her head briskly so that her beaded braids clicked together.

"Go ahead, girl," she said, "Orange before Blue."

We laughed, and the two of us pushed open the door and went out together.

Gwen walked beside me until we came to the hall leading to our social studies class. Then, without a word, she abandoned me and joined the other Blues. I understood. What had passed between us in the bathroom had had a tinge of conspiracy. Maybe Otero had set her up to it. But I preferred not to believe that. It was too easy to mistrust everyone in this game and I wanted to trust Gwen.

Adam, Troy, Dana, and the other Oranges and some Light Greens waited together, talking. The G4's watched but didn't stop them. I think we all expected Otero to bring the ax down on us as soon as class started. He could fine us, embarrass us, maybe fail us in the class. But it didn't seem to matter anymore.

You had to have an iron stomach to rise in the Color Game. You had to be nicer than nice, more willing to please than a child before

1 **to huddle with s.o.** *(American football)* to come close together as a group to discuss the next strategic move – 7 **top dog** person in the most influential position – 18 **sweeping** *weit ausholend* – 24 **to abandon** to leave behind – 26 **tinge** [tɪndʒ] trace – **conspiracy** [kən'spɪrəsɪ] making secret plans to do s.th. against the law – **to set s.o. up to s.th.** to make s.o. do s.th. that may be harmful to others – 32 **to fail s.o.** to declare that a student has not passed a test

Christmas, and so prideless that you'd bow and scrape to those you even resented. After a while you just didn't care anymore. You wanted to make waves *somehow,* so the injustices would be noticed and maybe righted. And if that didn't work, I didn't know what. When no one listens and hopelessness seems to have no end, how *do* people get rid of anger?

"In case you've all forgotten," Otero began when we'd all been seated, "today is the No-Tek beauty contest."

I let out my breath in relief. In my worry over how Otero might deal with us I'd almost forgotten about the contest. And instead of starting class with a tirade against the lower classes, Otero acted as if nothing had happened.

"Oh, boy," Adam groaned behind me. I reached a hand back to comfort him. His hand, always warm and firm, was icy.

"I notice the male population in class is quite a bit below normal," Otero said. "It will be interesting to hear the excuses for absence, tomorrow."

Without quite knowing how the contest would work, I felt uneasy for Adam and the rest of the males, the No-Teks. It seemed demeaning to be put on display for their body build and looks.

"To put this into perspective," Otero said, rubbing his beard. "Our No-Tek beauty contest is a ploy to open you men up. Most of you have no idea how sexist you really are. Nor how vulnerable women feel."

"Aw, come on. Women aren't helpless! It's the men who are! Women have all the power. They can say no," Justin cried.

"How often h[illegible] they said no, and men took advantage anyway!" Carol called out.

"If you're talking about rape, I think they ask for it ... the way they dress and act. ..."

"Booo!" The room rang with irate Teks jumping up and crying out at Justin. He put his hands up to his face, laughing, as if he expected to be clawed to death.

"All right ... all right! Enough. Let's see how the No-Teks feel when they're treated like females."

1 **to bow** [baʊ] **and scrape** to be extremely servile – 11 **tirade** ['taɪreɪd] a long angry speech – 19 **demeaning** causing a person to lose his/her sense of pride – 20 **to put on display** to exhibit – 22 **ploy** trick – **vulnerable** ['vʌlnərəbl] unprotected and therefore easily hurt – 29 **rape** the act of forcing s.o. to have sex – 31 **irate** [aɪ'reɪt] angry – 33 **to claw** [klɔ:] to tear or pull with claws *(Klauen)*

Otero had us move our chairs into a circle, leaving a large space in the middle. All the females, regardless of color, sat around the inner ring of the circle.

Of the sixteen boys normally in class, only ten had shown up. Brian made them stand at the door according to height, then turned on a tape recorder. We all began to laugh. The music coming from it belonged in a striptease show. Adam's face turned bright pink. Justin fidgeted. Juan and others struck sexy poses, rolling their pant legs up to expose their hairy legs, or standing with hands on hips and heads raised in their version of self-assured beauty queens

It was really funny, and pathetic, too, in a strange kind of way.

"All right, No-Teks. Get those gorgeous bods out there for the judges to see."

Juan really got into the spirit of the thing. He bumped and swayed to the suggestive music, and smiled seductively at each of us. Adam walked around with a forced smile on his face, as stiff as a board. Justin dug his hands into his pockets and slunk around, looking sullen. Almost strutting, Paul slowly unbuttoned his shirt down to his waist and grinned with pleasure at us.

"Way to go!" one of the girls called out.

"Look at those *buns!*"

"That one's getting a pot belly!"

"Come on, guys, don't bunch up like that. Let's see that gorgeous meat!"

I cringed, ashamed at some of the shouted commands, embarrassed to be part of this.

After a few turns around in the center of our circle about half the contestants were eliminated. They walked away, relieved, to sit behind us. Adam, Justin, Paul, Robert, and Juan remained.

"Hey, honey!" Carol sang out to Justin. "Don't hide it! We love the way you wear your pants. Open your shirt a bit more!"

Justin's face turned as red as a tomato. Reluctantly, he began doing what Carol asked. Some of the girls whistled like boys do. A couple

8 **to fidget** to move about restlessly – 10 **self-assured** sure of one's abilities – 12 **bods** *(slang)* bodies – 14 **to bump** to move the lower body forward as in a striptease show – **to sway** to move slowly from side to side – 15 **seductively** sexily – 16 **forced** not natural – 18 **sullen** silent and gloomy – **to strut** to walk proudly trying to look important – 21 **buns** *(AE slang)* bottom *(BE)* – 22 **pot belly** large stomach – 23 **to bunch up** to crowd together – 25 **to cringe** to move back or lower one's body in fear or shame – 32 **relunctantly** without any enthusiasm

of them sang. "Take it off ... take it off ..." cried the Teks in the rear. Justin tossed the shirt across the room and crossed his arms over his chest.

Adam started to laugh. He began unbuttoning his shirt and the others followed. Soon, all the No-Teks were marching around bare from the waist up. Paul rippled his impressive shoulder and arm muscles. Robert's hairy chest brought comments about ape ancestors. I wanted to run to Adam and put my arms around his strong tanned body.

The judging started. "Too flabby ... Boobs too big!" Justin was eliminated.

"No style. Robert, sit down."

"Bowlegged." Juan took a seat.

Soon, only Adam and Paul remained standing. Adam's face was flushed and he kept his arms crossed self-consciously over his bare chest.

"What's beauty without brains?" Mary asked. "For the final judging we'll be evaluating the remaining contestants on their intelligence and personality." Chairs were drawn up so that Adam and Paul faced the panel of G4's.

"How do you justify No-Teks' low threshold for pain?" Mary asked, reading from a card. "Is it biological?"

"Absolutely!" Paul said, grinning.

"Oh, come off it!" Adam protested. "Men can take pain just as well as women!"

The G4's conferred, then made marks on a sheet. Mary turned to the next question. "What about No-Teks' emotional outbursts? How come they can't control their emotions as well as Teks?"

"That's not true!" Adam exclaimed.

"Oh, sure it is," Paul said. "It's our hormones, you know." He winked at Adam.

A ripple of laughter went around the room. Some of the girls who came to class wearing baseball caps threw them in the air.

1 **rear** the back part – 5 **bare** without clothing – 6 **to ripple** to cause to move in small waves – 9 **flabby** too soft, not firm – **boobs** *(slang)* breasts – 12 **bowlegged** ['bəʊˌlegɪd] having legs that are bent outward *(O-beinig)* – 17 **to evaluate** to form an opinion of the value of s.th./s.o., to judge – 19 **panel** ['pænl] a group of people chosen to take part in or judge a contest – 20 **threshold** ['θreʃhəʊld] the lowest level at which s.th. begins to happen – 23 **Come off it!** Stop talking nonsense! – 26 **outburst** sudden powerful expression – 30 **to wink at s.o.** to open and shut one eye as a signal that what one says is not to be taken seriously – 31 **ripple** a sound as of flowing water

"One last question. Does the fact that Teks – women – can give the gift of life make you feel inferior?"

"Of course not!" Adam said. "Where would they be without our seed?"

Everyone booed him and Paul said, "Sure makes me feel inferior. What's a little old seed compared to the amazing experience of giving birth?"

"Thank you, No-Teks. You may leave the room while the judges make their decision."

In moments they were back. Adam looked bewildered, crushed. He must have realized Paul would win, but couldn't understand why.

Paul was properly crowned and draped with a scarlet satin cape while we sang the Miss America Pageant song. He took it well, grinning and chuckling, loving every bit of the attention.

"Well, how did that feel?" Otero asked next. "Justin? Still think women 'ask' for it?"

Justin mumbled something unintelligible.

Otero put a hand to his ear. "Say again?"

"I felt like a slab of beef!"

"Women feel that way a lot of the time!" Carol exclaimed.

"Yeah ... we can't walk down the street without you guys checking us out. You whistle and leer and practically salivate. How did you like *us* looking you over the way *you* do all the time?"

"How did you like being called 'honey', and having Carol put an arm around you?" Otero asked Adam.

"And how come you Teks haven't used your power all through the game to show the No-Teks what sexism is all about?" Mary challenged.

Questions and answers flew back and forth for the rest of the hour. Adam said he'd been made to feel "inferior" for the first time in his life. Justin admitted he'd never realized how men said and did things that could really hurt women. Several girls, including me, talked

4 **seed** *Samen* – 10 **bewildered** [bɪˈwɪldəd] confused – **crushed** humiliated *(erniedrigt)* – 12 **satin** [ˈsætn] material that is shiny on one side – 13 **Miss America Pageant** [ˈpædʒənt] **song** song that begins with "Here she comes, Miss America ..." sung when the winner has been chosen in the annual Miss America beauty contest – 14 **to chuckle** to laugh quietly – 17 **unintelligible** [ˌʌnɪnˈtelɪdʒɪbl] impossible to understand, unclear – 19 **slab** thick flat piece of s.th. – 21 **to check s.o. out** to examine s.o. to see how attractive this person is – 22 **to salivate** [ˈsælɪveɪt] *here: lüstern geifern*

about how hard it was for us to put down the No-Teks. It made us feel unfeminine.

When the class ended we walked out according to our color groups, still separated. But most of the talk went on. The girls giggled and whispered about how the boys looked and the boys seemed in a great hurry to get away.

Before we parted to go to our next class Adam said, "I don't know how to treat you anymore. Have I been very awful, very sexist?"

"On a scale of one to ten, ten being highest, you rate pretty high – about eight," I said, teasing.

"Eight?" He looked disappointed.

"Honey, it's very simple." I touched his cheek lovingly. "Just do unto me as you would have, et cetera, et cetera ... and you can't go far wrong."

His eyes crinkled into an amused smile. "Okay, okay. I get the idea. From now on I type my own papers."

1 **to put s.o. down** to make s.o. feel unimportant, to humiliate – 12 **"do unto me as you would have..."** reference to the Bible, Luke 6:31 i. e. treat others as you would like them to treat you – 15 **to crinkle** to cause to be covered with folds *(Falten)*

Chapter 14

I awoke Wednesday with a fluttery stomach. The rally meant so much to me. If we could pull it off, we'd have shown unity. We'd have proved that even being poor and downtrodden you might affect your own future.

Otero would try to stop us. Rumors had flown all over the school about that since Monday. And it did seem more than likely. The G4's had suddenly turned benign; it seemed almost as if they were biding their time. As if they had something big planned that didn't make harassing us worthwhile.

Mama was in the kitchen when I came down for breakfast. Usually, we sit quietly together, not talking, gazing out to the garden in the back of the house. In the very small yard Papa had created a feeling of space and peace. A few interesting black rocks nestled together on a bed of raked sand, like islands on a quiet sea. Azaleas and camellias grew against the back wall, with one early variety already in bloom.

Today, that view did nothing to ease my anxious stomach. I forced down juice and nibbled dry toast. Mama observed, but said nothing.

Gia was waiting for me on a corner, two blocks from school. She'd been promoted to Dark Green since the first time I'd tried to talk to her.

"Listen," she said, very excited. "I heard something's going on with the color armbands you guys made."

"I know, but do you know *what?*"

"I'm not sure, but is there any way for them to steal your stuff?" She glanced around, uneasily.

My stomach began to hurt. "I don't think so." To minimize the risk of the armbands disappearing we'd divided them up and stashed them in five different lockers. "No, I don't see how they could."

"Well, I just thought I'd tell you. I still feel allegiance to my old friends, the Light Greens, and they're in with you on this. Somehow, it's just not the same, being a Dark Green. Know what I mean?"

1 **fluttery** nervous, excited – 2 **to pull s.th. off** to succeed in doing s.th. – 3 **downtrodden** oppressed, badly treated – 5 **rumor** information that may not be true – 7 **benign** [bɪ'naɪn] kind, friendly – **to bide one's time** to wait until the right moment – 13 **to nestle together** to lie together – 14 **to rake** *harken* – **azalea** [ə'zeɪlɪə] a bush with colorful flowers – **camellia** [kə'mi:lɪə] Asian bush with rose-like flowers – 15 **in bloom** flowering – 27 **to stash** to hide – 29 **allegiance** [ə'li:dʒəns] loyalty

"I know. I'll be glad when it's Friday and we can sort all this out. I don't know if I can ever be friends with some guys, after the way they acted."

"Good luck."

Brian lounged against a wall watching everyone, watching us. "I feel like sticking my tongue out at him," Gia whispered. "Know what I mean?"

"Do it."

She giggled. Just as we passed him, we both stuck our tongues out at Brian. A dumb thing to do, but it really felt good.

The school bloomed with the banners and posters I'd lettered and Adam had helped color. During the night a team of Orange and Light Green No-Teks had put them up. For some reason the G4's were making no effort to have them removed.

The plan was to set up stations in five different parts of the school to hand out the bands before the bell rang for homeroom. Justin and Troy would stand nearby with the flyers, explaining what we believed, that we should help each other regardless of what color or sex or economic status we were. And the four-colored armbands represented that joining together.

I hurried to my locker to get the box of bands. At seven thirty I was supposed to be in front of the cafeteria, handing them out.

"Amy, wait!" I heard above the usual roar of early-morning talk out on the quad. Adam rushed toward me.

"Let's go to your locker."

"What's going on? You look funny."

He didn't answer my question, only hurried me along, up the stairs to the second-floor landing and my locker. Several boys leaned over the balustrade sailing paper airplanes.

"Open it," Adam said grimly.

Puzzled, I put my books down and fumbled with the combination, having to repeat the process because my fingers were as fluttery as my stomach.

As soon as I got the lock off, he almost pushed me out of the way. He opened the locker, glanced inside, then stepped aside. "Look."

5 **to lounge** [laʊndʒ] to stand leaning against s.th. in a lazy way – 16 **homeroom** *(AE)* the room where students are required to report before the start of lessons – 23 **roar** deep loud sound – 24 **quad** [kwɒd] quadrangle, i. e. courtyard between the buildings

"My pack! Where is it?"

"They took it. Those damn G4's. Otero must have gotten the combinations to our lockers from the office, and the G4's got here early and stole them! I'm so furious, I could kill!"

"But ... he'd have had to open *all* our lockers ... every one of us Oranges and Light Greens. ..."

"Unless .. unless we have a spy in our midst," Adam said. "Remember, someone alerted the G4's about our meeting at Juan's."

"Who?" I asked, and then, remembering the time, "The other lockers! What about them?"

"Empty, too."

"Oh, Adam ..." Angry tears sprang to my eyes. "Oh, Adam ..."

"Come on. We'll try to find the others and improvise something."

We ran down the hall and down the stairs, when I heard my name again. Gwen rushed toward us, pushing her way through the milling students.

"I heard what happened," she called out. "I'm sorry."

"Yeah ... sure." Adam pulled me along, making a path in the direction of the auditorium, our preset meeting place for emergencies.

"Wait," Gwen called, running after us. "I can help!"

"Adam!" I cried. "Slow down! Wait!" But he ignored me, still barreling through the crowd.

We found the students who should have been passing out the new armbands waiting, as well as other Oranges. "Otero's unfair! That's dirty pool! Now what are we going to do?"

"What are you doing here?" Juan asked Gwen. "Enjoying our failure?"

"Yeah," Justin added. "You have anything to do with this?"

"What's wrong with you creeps?" Gwen exclaimed. "You've become so paranoid you wouldn't trust your own mother. Otero's done a good job. He's shown you how powerless the lower classes really are!"

"So what did you come here for? To gloat?"

"Let's not argue, please?" I pleaded. "Gwen thinks she can help. We've only got fifteen minutes before school starts. Stop arguing and listen!"

4 **furious** very angry – 7 **spy** a person sent to find out secrets about s.o. – 8 **to alert** [ə'lɜ:t] to warn, to draw s.o.'s attention to a possible danger, etc. – 19 **preset** arranged beforehand – 21 **to barrel** *(AE slang)* to move at high speed – 25 **dirty pool** *(informal)* unfair play – 33 **to gloat** to feel happy about the misfortunes of others

"Sure, like what could *you* do?"

"Well, if you feel like that ..." Gwen's lips tightened. She clutched a heavy shopping bag in both hands. "Bye bye, guys."

"Gwen ..."

She shook off my arm. "It's just the way Otero says. People *don't* look beyond labels. Even when the upper classes want to help, no one figures they're for real."

"Gwen, please, tell us what you had in mind. We're desperate." I flashed a warning scowl at Justin, who had shown such suspicion at Gwen's motives. "Gwen, please ..."

She hesitated, then turned back to us. "Okay ... but only for you, Amy." She put the heavy bag on the ground and dug into it. Out came a big roll of cheap red ribbon. "Your armbands." She smiled triumphantly. "I've got rolls and rolls of this stuff. Scissors, too. Cost me bucks ... but I figure you white dudes will be happy to reimburse me."

"Red?" someone asked doubtfully.

"Red. Why not? It's the color of revolution. Besides, it was the only color I could get at the price."

"What are we supposed to do with the stuff?"

"Where's your imagination, you Orange No-Tek? Man, I can't believe this." She dipped into the bag again, removing cheap shears, the kind used in kindergartens. "This is what you do, man. You measure out a length like this. You cut like this. And you hand it to a student to tie around the arm. *Comprende?*"

"That's brilliant!" I exclaimed, anxious to forestall the nasty reply I saw forming in some of the faces around us. "Let's get going! We only have fifteen minutes before the bell rings."

I began handing out rolls of ribbon and in a matter of minutes our team dispersed to the far corners of the school. We had fifteen minutes to cut and pass out a lot of ribbon – ribbon we hoped would tie the whole student body together.

The rally succeeded beautifully. We couldn't cut ribbons fast enough. Everyone wanted them. The only holdouts, Blues and Dark Greens,

2 **to clutch** to hold tightly – 13 **ribbon** ['rɪbən] a narrow strip of cloth – 15 **bucks** *(AE slang)* a lot of money – **to reimburse** [ˌriːɪm'bɜːs] to pay back – 21 **to dip into** to put one's hand into s.th. to take s.th. out – **shears** [ʃɪəz] large scissors – 24 **Comprende?** [kəm'prendeɪ] *(Spanish)* Do you understand? – 25 **to forestall** [fɔː'stɔːl] to prevent s.o. from doing s.th. by acting first – 33 **holdout** person who refuses to co-operate

became the oddballs. Except they got to wear our ribbons, too ... pinned to their backs without their knowing.

Afterwards, we went around congratulating ourselves and hugging each other. "We did it! The whole school's behind us! Down with color differences!"

Otero didn't seem a bit upset. High on our success we came to class smiling like Cheshire cats. Nothing he said or the G4's did could hurt us now.

"You've pulled off what no other class did before," Otero said. "Congratulations. Social and value changes are what this game is all about. Only don't celebrate yet. By tomorrow you might be right back to where you were. Or will you have reached a higher level of understanding, where you see each other not as colors, but as human beings?"

Adam tapped me on the shoulder and whispered, "Boy, is he going to be surprised. We're all equal; no one can make us feel otherwise again." I grinned back at him and nodded.

The G4's started in with their fines, coming down heavy on us Oranges. Gwen was demoted. Troy, for no reason we could figure, was promoted. But none of it touched us. We were still too high. No matter what Otero said, we'd succeeded in uniting the Oranges and Light Greens, in getting the help of a Blue defector. We'd proven that if you unite against injustice you *can* bring about change.

Friday morning, the last day of the Color Game, Mama hung around the kitchen longer than usual. I'd been babbling about my friends, trying to figure out who might be the spy, going on about Adam and how he'd been treating me lately. She kept checking the clock, but didn't leave for work. Finally, I stopped talking long enough to realize Mama felt uneasy about something.

"Mama?" I asked, right out. "What's wrong?"

She gave me this little embarrassed shrug and poured another cup of tea for herself, making a little ceremony of it before answering. Finally she said, "This boy Adam. He sounds like a good boy. He seems to care a great deal about you."

I blushed. "Yes, Mama. And I care about him, too."

1 **oddball** person who is noticeably different from the usual – 7 **Cheshire** ['tʃeʃə] **cat** like the grinning Cheshire cat in Lewis Carroll's (1832-1898) *Alice in Wonderland* – 22 **defector** person who changes loyalties and joins the opposition – **proven** ['pru:vn] *(AE)* proved *(BE)*

"I can see that." Mama shook her head and gazed out at the garden, the cup held in both hands. "Perhaps Papa and I have been wrong."

I swallowed and waited for her to go on.

"It is hard to say. It is different now than when we were young. ..." Again she paused. "Papa says ... it is only proper that you ask Adam to have dinner with us after all this time."

"Papa says?"

"Yes, Papa." She gave me a small, embarrassed smile. "He is not such a cold man as you think. He sees how you feel. He tries to understand."

"Mama, when?" I asked, heart beating rapidly. I could hardly wait to get to school to tell Adam.

"Sunday. Hideo and Sue will be here. We will sit in the garden and then we will have dinner. All of us, together."

"Oh, Mama!" I cried, jumping up. "Oh, Mama, Mama, Mama! I love you!" I hugged her from behind and went dancing around the kitchen, already making plans about what to wear and how I'd tell Adam.

Otero had the chairs in the room set up in a circle on this, the last day of the game. Even so, out of habit, out of a sense of our own unity, we chose seats near others of our color.

"Today," he announced, "we remove our color bands and life goes back to normal. I want you all to remember that some people can't ever take off their armbands. Just because of their color they'll be treated with less respect than others all of their lives. Except, maybe not by those who have been part of this game."

"Was the assignment of colors rigged?" someone called out.

Otero smiled. "Yes and no. Remember the questionnaires you filled out about a week before we started the game? Well that's how we learned of your general economic status and attitudes. Those answers helped us – me and the G4's – to decide who should become what. After all, the purpose of the game is to learn what it's like for others, those less fortunate or more fortunate than you."

"But how did you work it?" Justin asked. "We picked the color chips ourselves."

21 **out of habit** because one is so used to doing s.th. – 28 **assignment** [ə'saɪnmənt] the way s.th. is given out – 36 **chip** a small thin round piece of plastic often used for games

"Yes you did, but what you didn't know is that we had double bags. One held the chips for the upper classes and one for the lower classes. When you reached into the bags, the G4 held open only one of the two. That way your choices were halved. We couldn't rig it more precisely than that, and there were some random – Juan, for example."

A groan went through the class and the G4's chuckled as if they'd put something over on us.

"Whenever we thought someone wasn't learning enough in a particular color, the G4's and I voted to promote or demote. Remember how Carol was promoted to Blue? It was because as a Dark Green she wasn't learning anything. We could tell from her journal. As a Blue she found how nice it was to be respected and not be harassed, so she did everything she could to make Blue."

"I was just playing the game the way it works in real life!" Carol protested in defense.

Otero tugged at his beard. "Before we give up our bands, is there anything you'd like to say about your experience, good or bad?"

Brian spoke first. "I want to apologize for being so mean to a lot of you. I did it for the game. I'm really a very nice guy!" Catcalls and cries of disbelief filled the air and I found myself wondering how many other G4's and Blues really enjoyed their power, despite their protests.

"Boy, was I pissed off when Gwen stopped me after gym last week," Rob said. "She looked me up and down with this little smirk on her face and says, 'You oughta wear shorts more often, Rob. Ya' got nice legs.' "

Some of the girls laughed uncomfortably, but Rob went on, "I never really thought how we guys treat girls until then. I started to think how I treat my girlfriend and didn't like what I was finding." His voice cracked with emotion. "I was so ... paternalistic!"

Adam leaned toward me and whispered, "I feel like putting an arm around him, if it wouldn't be misunderstood."

"I just hated being Orange," Michelle said. "My best friend ignored me through the whole game. It really made me think. Until this game I never really noticed anyone who was poor or a different color from me."

5 **random** without any plan or method – 7 **to put s.th. over s.o.** to trick, to deceive – 13 **to make s.th.** *here:* to be promoted to s.th. – 16 **to tug** to pull – 19 **catcalls** loud whistles or shouts to show displeasure – 22 **gym** [dʒɪm] *here:* gymnastics *(Turnen)* – 23 **smirk** a self-satisfied smile, often because of s.o.'s misfortune – 24 **oughta** *(slang)* ought to – **Ya'** *(slang)* you have – 29 **paternalistic** [---'--] authoritarian in a good-natured way, like a father

"Now I know why ethnic groups stick together," Adam said. "It's because there's safety in being with your own, especially when society separates people into 'them' and 'us.' "

"Why, Adam," Paul joked. "You did learn something!"

"You all learned something," Otero said. "I hope what you learned sticks with you all your lives, because if it does, the world will be a better place to live in."

"Who was the spy?" I called out.

"You didn't guess?" Otero smiled. "I want you all to know he spied for us – me and the G4's – on orders, so don't hold it against him. If he'd like to identify himself, it's up to him."

"Who?" several of us called out. I began to suspect everyone. Otero spoke of a *him,* so it could be Juan, Robert, Justin, even Adam.

Troy stood up.

Adam and I exchanged shocked glances. "Troy? But he ..."

He grinned a crooked smile. "I only did what I was told."

"You spied on us! You leaked our plans to the G4's so they'd raid us at Juan's? You told them which lockers had the armbands? You threw suspicion on Juan and Amy! *Troy!*"

"Aw, come on," he protested. "You learned something, didn't you?"

Otero held up a hand. "We're running late and I have some things to say before the *hugging.*" The class quieted immediately. Otero leaned across his desk. "I promised to take you on a journey to another planet where color and social status were regulated by the armbands you wore. Soon you're going to remove those bands. I hope you'll remember the feelings you had these past weeks of associating people's character with their band color. That's what's called *stereotyping.* You found yourselves looking at a person's band first, then you knew how to interact with that person." Otero's voice dropped as if he were choked with emotion.

"Remember how that felt *forever,* because that's how it is in real life, only people don't look at armbands. They look at skin color, or facial features, or listen to accents, or judge others by the way they dress, not by the kind of people they are!"

He cleared his throat. "In a moment you'll remove your color

16 **crooked** ['krʊkɪd] twisted – 17 **to leak** to make known facts that should be kept secret – **to raid** to suddenly attack or visit a place, especially to find stolen goods

bands, but think how many people can't remove theirs – their skin color, or the labels of poverty."

I felt very close to Mr. Otero at that moment and think everyone in the room felt the same. Adam squeezed my hand.

"I've said my piece, now it's time to heal whatever hurts you may have brought to others or felt because of others." Otero moved to the front of the room. The G4's took positions to his left. "You'll each come forward, throw your color band on the floor, then exchange hugs so there are no hard feelings. First you'll hug me, then each of the G4's, then stand at the end of the line so each person in turn will hug each other. Blues first."

After that the room became noisy and confused. Paul, a head taller than Otero, acted as if he didn't know how to hug men, making everybody laugh. Otero whispered a few words to Gwen and she whispered back, then they hugged each other. Others, like Carol, got weepy as they passed from Otero to each of the G4's, and down the line past those who had come before.

When it was my turn, my heart began thumping like a Fourth of July band and my throat swelled with emotion. I dropped my orange and blue bands on the small mountain of bands on the floor, then stepped up to Otero. Without a word we hugged each other with special warmth. "I'm very proud of you, Amy. You're a born leader. And you lead with a gentle hand."

"Thanks, Mr. Otero," I whispered.

Brian opened his arms to me as I moved along to the G4's. "Amy ..."

"Yeah?" I said, touching hands but not moving into his embrace.

"I hope there are no hard feelings."

"Oh, no. Hardly any."

He chuckled. "If you're not tied down to that dumb Orange No-Tek, I'd still like to see you."

"Not a chance," Adam said, answering for me.

Bad habits die slowly, I guess. "Nothing's impossible, Brian," I said, answering for myself. "Just look at what we Oranges accomplished."

"You're putting me on."

5 **piece** what was planned to be said – **to heal** to make well again – 15 **weepy** starting to cry – 18 **Fourth of July** American national holiday, often celebrated with parades and marching bands – 35 **to put s.o. on** to play a trick on, to deceive

I raised an eyebrow, enigmatically, and moved on. Brian looked after me and I winked, feeling a silly self-conscious grin start at my lips.

The last few minutes of the class we milled around some more, talking about our feelings. Carol came up to me, teary-eyed and a little apprehensive. "I'm so glad it's over. Still friends?"

Of course we were, even more so. I felt a glow of love for everyone in class. We'd shared so much. It would be strange to leave the room without my color band, to go back to how it was before.

"Do you feel any different?" Adam asked as we left together.

"Yes ... kind of subdued." Blues and Dark Greens and Light Greens went by, touching us as they passed. "I've come to like people I didn't know before, like Gwen. Do you think ... I mean, let's ask her to sit at our lunch table."

Adam noticed the midsentence switch and smiled. "Sure – Juan, too."

I squeezed his hand. "By the way, doing anything Sunday? Mama and Papa invited you to dinner." Butterflies again, even though I couldn't imagine Adam saying no. For a second I thought of Mrs. Tarcher and the ugly feelings she brought out in me. Then I figured, if she doesn't like me, it's *her* problem.

"So?"

Adam's eyes twinkled, but he said, "I don't know. Depends on the menu."

"Oh?" My hackles went up. Would I always be on guard? "If you're worried about what you're likely to eat, it will probably be roast beef and potatoes."

"That's just it," Adam said. "I was hoping for sushi, tempura, or something interesting like that." He tilted his head and gave me a tender, intimate smile. "I can eat roast beef and potatoes any time."

"Adam ..." I said. "Adam Tarcher ..." My throat filled with happy tears. We faced each other in the middle of the crowded hallway, kids going by us on both sides, and smiled. "I'll talk to the chef," I said.

5 **apprehensive** [ˌæprɪˈhensɪv] anxious – 7 **glow** warm feeling – 11 **subdued** [səbˈdjuːd] unnaturally quiet – 15 **switch** sudden change – 23 **to twinkle** to shine like a star – 24 **menu** [ˈmenjuː] dishes that will be served – 25 **my hackles went up** *(idiom)* I became angry – 28 **sushi** [ˈsuːʃɪ] Japanese meal of rice cakes and raw fish – **tempura** [temˈpuːrə] Japanese fried seafood – 33 **chef** [ʃef] head cook

Material for Further Study

1. America: A Society with a Rigid Class System?

It is perhaps ironic that a society such as that of the United States, which emphasizes equality and democracy, has such a separation between and among classes and that classes provide their members such different experiences. Nevertheless, social interaction across class lines tends to be either sporadic or superficial, or both. The reason is partly the financial differences from one class to the next. Large, expensive homes are effectively prohibited to the lower classes. This means that lower- and upper-class neighborhoods will be separated, which in turn means that children of different classes will not meet and play with each other. To the extent that schools serve neighborhoods or that wealthier children attend private schools, children will continue to be separated during school years. Should they meet through a device such as busing, they will still not necessarily socialize beyond the superficial level required by attending the same school. Their parents will by definition be engaged in different kinds of work, so they will not likely meet, either. And while all of these people are separated, they will be living, working, and playing with very little input from other classes. In short, all aspects of their lives, from the most important to the most trivial, will develop in relative isolation and, therefore, in different directions. And whatever that development is, it will be passed from one generation to the next. A growing child learns to shoot craps, go bowling, or play polo not by choice but rather by doing whatever activity is prevalent in his or her social environment. The same is true of modes of speaking, ways of worship-

rigid fixed, unable to change – 5 **sporadic** [spəˈrædɪk] happening only occasionally – **superficial** [su:pəˈfɪʃl]] *oberflächlich* – 9 **in turn** *here:* as a result – 10 **to the extent** as much as – 13 **device** *here:* special plan or program – **busing** a system of sending poorer children, especially Blacks, to schools attended by wealthier children, which was started by the government in the 1960s – 15 **to be engaged in** *here:* to be employed in – 18 **input** *here:* exchange of ideas, information – 22 **to shoot craps** to play a gambling game in which dice *(Würfel)* are thrown – 23 **prevalent** [ˈprevələnt] most widespread, most common – 24 **mode** way – **ways of worshiping** (*BE* worshipping) *here:* the kinds of churches one goes to ing, attitudes toward education, and so on. As differences develop through isolation, so they persist through isolation.

When individuals do meet across classes, they usually become uncomfortable in the face of their differences and they retreat. The classes into which they retreat are ready-made environments for group formation. When class membership is permanent (that is, determined for life), groups formed from the common experience of that class will also be permanent. But that, of course, is not the case in the United States. It is very easy to drop down in class in the United States (unless you are already on the bottom), and it is possible (although often difficult) to move up. In a society where individuals change classes, their groups will also change as their new classes give them new interests and experiences. A longshoreman who becomes a published author or a chorus girl who becomes the star of the show will probably find old friends drifting away with old interests, to be replaced by new friends who fit in better with present concerns.

From *Race and Ethnic Relations: The Social and Political Experience of Minority Groups* by Reid Luhman and Stuart Gilman, Belmont; CA: Wadsworth Publishing Company, 1980, pp. 56–57.

2. An Outsider in the Slums

The following is an extract from Down These Mean Streets, *the autobiography of an American of Puerto Rican descent who grew up in the slums of New York in the 1960s.*

Sometimes you don't fit in like if you're Puerto Rican on an Italian block. After my new baby brother, Ricardo, died of some kind of germs, Poppa moved from 111th Street to Italian turf on 114th Street

26 **persist** to continue without changing – 28 **to retreat** to return to where one has come from – 37 **longshoreman** *(AE)* person whose job it is to load and unload ships – 38 **chorus** ['kɔ:rəs] **girl** woman who dances or sings in a group in musicals or shows – 39 **to drift away** *here:* to slowly end a relationship – 40 **concerns** things that are interesting or important
2 **block** *(AE) here:* the length of a street from one crossing to another in a city – 3 **germs** bacteria or viruses – **Poppa** *(informal)* father – **111th Street** the area mentioned here is on the upper East Side of New York City – **turf** [tɜ:f] *(informal)* one's own territory

between Second and Third Avenue. I guess Poppa wanted to get Momma away from the hard memories of the old pad.

I sure missed 111th Street, where everybody acted, walked, and talked like me. But on 114th Street everything went all right for a while. There were a few dirty looks from the spaghetti-an'-sauce cats, but no big sweat. Till that one day I was on my way home from school and almost had reached my stoop when someone called: "Hey, you dirty fuckin' spic."

The words hit my ears and almost made me curse Poppa at the same time. I turned around real slow and found my face pushing in the finger of an Italian kid about my age. He had five or six of his friends with him.

"Hey, you," he said. "What nationality are ya?"

I looked at him and wondered which nationality to pick. And one of his friends said, "Ah, Rocky, he's black enuff to be a nigger. Ain't that what you is, kid?"

My voice was almost shy in its anger. "I'm Puerto Rican," I said. "I was born here." I wanted to shout it, but it came out like a whisper.

"Right here inna street?" Rocky sneered. "Ya mean right here inna middle of da street?"

They all laughed.

I hated them. I shook my head slowly from side to side. "Uh-uh," I said softly. "I was born inna hospital – inna bed."

"Umm, *paisan* – born inna bed," Rocky said.

I didn't like Rocky Italiano's voice. "Inna hospital," I whispered, and all the time my eyes were trying to cut down the long distance from this trouble to my stoop. But it was no good; I was hemmed in by Rocky's friends. I couldn't help thinking about kids getting wasted for moving into a block belonging to other people.

"What hospital, *paisan?*" Bad Rocky pushed.

5 **pad** *(informal)* apartment, flat – 8 **spaghetti-an'-sauce cats** *(AE slang)* Italians – 9 **no big sweat** *(AE slang)* nothing to get upset about – 10 **stoop** small platform with steps at the entrance of a house – 11 **spic** *(AE slang, derogatory)* Puerto Rican – 12 **to curse** to complain angrily using rude language – 13 **real** *(AE informal)* very – 16 **ya** *(slang)* you – 18 **enuff** *(slang)* enough – **ain't** *(slang)* isn't – 22 **inna** *(slang)* in the – **to sneer** to smile or speak in a way that shows you don't think much of another person – 23 **da** *(slang)* the – 25 **uh-uh** *(slang)* no – 27 **paisan** [paɪ'zɑ:n] *(Italian)* peasant, i.e. stupid person – 30 **to hem s.o. in** to surround s.o. and make it impossible for that person to move away – 31 **to get wasted** *(informal)* to get killed

"Harlem Hospital," I answered, wishing like all hell that it was 5 o'clock instead of just 3 o'clock, 'cause Poppa came home at 5. I looked around for some friendly faces belonging to grown-up people, but the elders were all busy yakking away in Italian. I couldn't help thinking how much like Spanish it sounded. Shit, that should make us something like relatives.

"Harlem Hospital?" said a voice. "I knew he was a nigger."

"Yeah," said another voice from an expert on color. "That's the hospital where all them black bastards get born at."

3. White as Black

The following extract from Black Like Me *describes the experiences of a white man in the late 1950s who passed as a Black by dying his skin (cf.* The War Between the Classes *p. 72).*

Finally, after I gave up hope and decided I must remain in New Orleans without funds until the banks opened on Monday, I walked toward town. Small gold-lettering on the window of a store caught my attention: CATHOLIC BOOK STORE. Knowing the Catholic stand on racism, I wondered if this shop might cash a Negro's check. With some hesitation, I opened the door and entered. I was prepared to be disappointed.

"Would you cash a twenty-dollar traveler's check for me?" I asked the proprietress.

"Of course," she said without hesitation, as though nothing could be more natural. She did not even study me.

I was so grateful I bought a number of paperbook books [...]. With these in my jacket, I hurried toward the Greyhound bus station.

34 **like all hell** *(informal)* very much – 35 **'cause** *(slang)* because – 37 **to yak** *(informal)* to talk a lot about unimportant matters – 41 **yeah** [jeə] *(slang)* yes – 42 **bastard** *(slang, derogatory)* nasty person

2 **funds** money – 5 **to cash a check** (*BE* cheque) to give s.o. money in return for a check – 9 **proprietress** [prəʊ'praɪətrəs] female owner – 13 **Greyhound** bus company

In the bus station lobby, I looked for signs indicating a colored waiting room, but saw none. I walked up to the ticket counter. When the lady ticket-seller saw me, her otherwise attractive face turned sour, violently so. This look was so unexpected and so unprovoked I was taken aback.

"What do you want?" she snapped.

Taking care to pitch my voice to politeness, I asked about the next bus to Hattiesburg.

She answered rudely and glared at me with such loathing I knew I was receiving what the Negroes call "the hate stare." It was my first experience with it. It is far more than the look of disapproval one occasionally gets. This was so exaggeratedly hateful I would have been amused if I had not been so surprised.

I framed the words in my mind: "Pardon me, but have I done something to offend you?" But I realized I had done nothing – my color offended her.

"I'd like a one-way ticket to Hattiesburg, please," I said and placed a ten-dollar bill on the counter.

"I can't change that big a bill," she said abruptly and turned away, as though the matter were closed. I remained at the window, feeling strangely abandoned but not knowing what else to do. In a while she flew back at me, her face flushed, and fairly shouted: "I *told* you – I can't change that big a bill."

"Surely," I said stiffly, "in the entire Greyhound system there must be some means of changing a ten-dollar bill. Perhaps the manager –"

She jerked the bill furiously from my hand and stepped away from the window. In a moment she reappeared to hurl my change and the ticket on the counter with such force most of it fell on the floor at my feet. I was truly dumbfounded by this deep fury that possessed her whenever she looked at me. Her performance was so venomous, I felt sorry for her. It must have shown in my expression, for her face con-

14 **colored** *here:* for Blacks – 18 **to be taken aback** to be shocked – 20 **to pitch** *here:* to adjust – 22 **rudely** impolitely – **to glare** to stare in an unfriendly way – **loathing** hatred – 27 **to frame** to formulate – 28 **to offend** to hurt s.o.'s feelings – 31 **bill** *(AE)* banknote – 34 **abandoned** left alone, deserted – 35 **flushed** red with anger – 39 **to jerk** to take with a sudden movement – 40 **to hurl** to throw violently – 42 **dumbfounded** [dʌmˈfaʊndɪd] speechless because of being astonished – **fury** [ˈfjʊərɪ] great anger – 43 **venomous** [ˈvenəməs] extremely bitter – 44 **to congest** *here:* to become filled with blood

gested to high pink. She undoubtedly considered it a supreme insolence for a Negro to dare to feel sorry for her.

[...]

Again, an important part of my daily life was spent searching for the basic things that all whites take for granted: a place to eat, or somewhere to find a drink of water, a rest room, somewhere to wash my hands. More than once I walked into drugstores where a Negro can buy cigarettes or anything else except soda fountain service. I asked politely where I might find a glass of water. Though they had water not three yards away, they carefully directed me to the nearest Negro café. Had I asked outright for a drink, they would perhaps have given it. But I never asked. The Negro dreads rejection, and I waited for them to offer the drink. Not one ever did. No matter where you are, the nearest Negro café is always far away, it seems. I learned to eat a great deal when it was available and convenient, because it might not be available or convenient when the belly next indicated its hunger. I have been told that many distinguished Negroes whose careers have brought them South encounter similar difficulties. All the honors in the world cannot buy them a cup of coffee in the lowest greasy-spoon joint. It is not that they crave service in the white man's café over their own – it is simply that in many sparsely settled areas Negro cafés do not exist; and even in the densely settled areas, one must sometimes cross town for a glass of water. It is rankling, too, to be encouraged to buy all of one's goods in white stores and then be refused soda-fountain or rest-room service.

No, it makes no sense, but in so far as the Negro is concerned, nothing makes much sense.

Excerpt from *Black Like Me* by John Howard Griffin, New York:

45 **high** *here:* bright – **supreme** extreme – **insolence** extremely disrespectful behavior – 48 **to take s.th. for granted** to consider s.th. to be quite normal – 49 **rest room** *(AE)* toilet – 51 **soda fountain** *(AE)* a counter in a drugstore where one is served soft drinks, ice-cream, a cup of coffee, a sandwich, etc. – 54 **outright** openly – 55 **to dread** [dred] to fear – **rejection** being refused – 59 **belly** *(informal)* stomach – 60 **distinguished** [dɪ'stɪŋgwɪʃt] famous and respected – 61 **to encounter** to meet with, to experience – 62 **greasy-spoon joint** *(AE slang)* cheap and dirty restaurant – 63 **to crave s.th. over another thing** to prefer s.th. very much more than another thing – 64 **sparsely** ['spɑ:slɪ] **settled** with few inhabitants – 67 **rankling** irritating, causing bitterness and resentment

4. How the Students Reacted to the Experiment

"Watching the harassment of the Oranges reminds me of the time when my brother and I were 2 of 4 blacks in a student population of 700–900. As it is OK ... for the upper classes to call the lower classes names and do other things, so it was OK for those students to call us what they pleased. The teachers would allow this because they saw it as allowable; except when we called the other students a name or used any form of retaliation. It was too obviously one-sided."

Dark Green No-Tek, 1985.
(A black person)

"As an Orange, I was labeled deviant by the Color Game society. Therefore, I was deviant. This belief manifested itself most conspicuously in the bond that pulled Oranges together. Gang-like, we had no one but each other. And yet my inferior position in society affected my personal actions as well. When I walked around campus, I kept my eyes on the ground, hoping to remain invisible. I took to dining alone at the end of meals, eating quickly, in an attempt to get back to my 'territory' (my room) before an upper-class man could catch me. I found myself getting angry at other Oranges for not following rules – for not remaining invisible. In other words, I let the stereotypical beliefs against the Oranges in the Color Game society influence my actions.

Orange Tek, 1985.
(A white person)

"... the emotional recognition of the political implication of what it meant for a No-Tek to type a paper written by a Tek on the subject of Tek superiority. I thought, 'My God! Women have been doing this shit for centuries.' 'This shit' being: doing the research for their male counterparts who receive the credit and prestige for what are frequently works perpetuating the ideology of women's inferior position.

1 **harassment** [hə'ræsmənt] continuously troubling and annoying s.o. – 7 **retaliation** act of repaying an injury or insult with a similar one – 8 **to label** to classify, to stick a "label" on s.o. – **deviant** ['di:vɪənt] not behaving normally – 9 **to manifest** ['mænɪfest] to show clearly, to demonstrate – **conspicuously** very noticeably – 10 **bond** link, tie – 12 **campus** the grounds of a school or university – 13 **to take to doing s.th.** to begin to do s.th. regularly – 19 **implication** possible later effect – 23 **counterpart** *Gegenstück* – 22 **research** [rɪ'sɜ:tʃ] careful study to find out facts about s.th. – 24 **to perpetuate** [pə'petʃʊeɪt] to cause s.th. to continue

The effect of this realization was: What the heck am I typing this offensive shit about my own inferiority … and SLAM! A wall hit me at about a hundred miles an hour."

Dark Green/Orange No-Tek, 1984.
(A white person)

"I'm so confused now. I want to move up – I always have. But I don't want to jeopardize losing what I have as a Light Green. Being a low life ain't so bad if you know how to handle it. In a way, Light Greens are sort of above G4's and Blues in that they need us a lot more than we need them … I've decided that no matter what happens to me, I'll still remain loyal to my class. I guess I'm building Light Green pride."

Light Green No-Tek, 1985.
(A Jewish person)

"Today I will find out how I can help the lower colors without losing my Dark Greenness. I guess this sounds a bit contradictory. I feel that I can help more as a more powerful, more affluent color. And this is the way I see it in the real world."

Dark Green Tek, 1985.
(A Puerto Rican person)

"When I picked my blue armband, a tremendous sense of power came over me. I relaxed … I immediately felt it important to exercise my power and authority. In the beginning, I encountered astonished looks from the lower classes who had to respond to my commands through the initial weeks. It was significant that I didn't view my actions as requests but rather as commands. It was their duty and my right to expect that they perform to my wants and needs."

Blue No-Tek, 1984.
(A black person)

From documentation provided by Ray Otero. Reprinted by permission of Raymond M. Otero, Santurce, Puerto Rico.

25 **heck** *(slang)* harmless word for "hell" – **offensive** hurting s.o.'s feelings – 26 **slam** loud noise such as of a door being violently shut – 29 **to jeopardize** ['dʒepədaɪz] to put in danger, to risk – 30 **to handle s.th.** to deal with s.th. – 35 **contradictory** *widersprüchlich* – 36 **affluent** ['æflʊənt] wealthy – 38 **tremendous** great – 39 **to exercise** to use – 40 **to encounter** to experience – 42 **initial** [ɪ'nɪʃl] first few

5. Player Finds 'Color Game' Far Too Real

Ray Otero didn't know what he was getting into.

Ten years ago, the sociology instructor at Occidental College developed an innovative approach to teaching about racism through a role-playing exercise he called "The Color Game."

Six years later, a documentary on the game produced by a Los Angeles television station won an Emmy and four years after that, "CBS Schoolbreak Special" based on the game aired nationally. But now Otero – and the very premise of his controversial sociological experiment – are under attack.

Gabrielle Sanchez-Goyene, a 13-year-old junior at Holy Family High School in Glendale, was asked to play a version of the game as part of a social justice class last November. In December, after playing the game for one day, she filed a $2.1-million lawsuit against the parochial school and the Los Angeles Archdiocese, claiming emotional damage. Last week, spurred by reports that Otero closely advised the high school teacher who taught the game, an attorney for the Sanchez-Goyen family said they will name the professor as a defendant in the suit as well.

Otero, a mild-mannered native of Puerto Riceo with an almost missionary zeal for improving relations between the races, seems perplexed by all the fuss.

"I have no complaints about 'The Color Game,' except this one time, this one day," Otero said. "It's so unfair. Judging the game by playing for one day is like judging a book by reading the first page."

[...]

Otero says the point of the game is to make participants realize the absurdity of judging others based solely on their external labels or characteristics by living through such experiences themselves.

2 **Occidental College** small university in Los Angeles – 3 **innovative** ['ɪnəveɪtɪv] introducing a new idea – 6 **Emmy** annual award given to outstanding programs on TV – **CBS** one of the major private TV networks in America – 7 **to air** to broadcast – 8 **premise** ['premɪs] theoretical basis – 11 **Glendale** suburb of Los Angeles – 13 **to file a lawsuit against** *verklagen* – 14 **parochial** [pə'rəʊkɪəl] **school** a private (usually Roman Catholic) school – **archdiocese** [ˌɑːtʃ'daɪəsɪs] *Erzdiözese* – 15 **to spur** to encourage, to stimulate – 16 **attorney** [ə'tɜːnɪ] *Rechtsanwalt* – 17 **defendant** person in a lawcourt who is accused or sued – 19 **mild-mannered** quiet and polite – 20 **zeal** [ziːl] great enthusiasm – **perplexed** puzzled, confused – 21 **fuss** excitement or activity – 26 **solely** only – **label** description consisting of one or a few words

At Holy Family, playing the game was mandatory for students in the class. Sanchez-Goyen, an "A" student who skipped three grades, drew the lowest color – orange. After one day of play, she quit the game. Soon after, she left the school and soon after that, she and her parents filed suit.

Looking back on his involvement at Holy Family, Otero acknowledges he may have made a serious mistake.

"If I had it to do over again, I would insist that it not be mandatory, that it be an elective," Otero said.

28 **mandatory** compulsory, demanded or required by those in authority – 29 **"A" student** a student who has the highest grade in all subjects – **to skip a grade** *überspringen (Klasse)* – 30 **to draw, drew, drawn** to get by chance – **to quit** to leave – 33 **involvement** part in s.th., having to do with s.th. – **to acknowledge** to admit – 36 **elective** course or subject that can be taken if one wants to